To Terry?
All my best —
anne Leftier
oct 2014
2-27-25

WestBow Press books may be ordered through booksellers or by contacting:

WestBow Press
A Division of Thomas Nelson & Zondervan
1663 Liberty Drive
Bloomington, IN 47403
www.westbowpress.com
1 (866) 928-1240

ISBN: 978-1-9736-7375-0 (sc)
ISBN: 978-1-9736-7377-4 (hc)
ISBN: 978-1-9736-7376-7 (e)

Library of Congress Control Number: 2019913163

Print information available on the last page.

WestBow Press rev. date: 09/23/2019

OTHER BOOKS

Walking with John XXIII

Contents

Dedication

To my Pirate, who has walked the plank with me for forty-two years.

Readers' Comments

A unique read giving readers the perspective of what it's like to go from West Coast living to small town southern living, where thoughts and opinions are not what Anne Jeffries is accustomed to.

-Krista Zavala

Thoughtful visits of a vagabond soul.

-Biene Vallee

"Travel along with Anne on her bittersweet and inspiring journey. You will laugh and maybe cry a bit too'"

-TBeth

Anne is delightful to read as she shares her experiences with both the eye of an artist and a sense of wonder and reflection.

- ERJ

Acknowledgments

Many thanks to Toni and Biene who never stopped encouraging me to follow my dreams; to Michelle Hillerman and Marie Lily Roberson who taught me how to be brave; to Caryn Setterquist who walked me through some very dark technical moments; to Christine Sides-Williams who welcomed my musings on life in the Bootheel to the pages of the *Pemiscot Press;* to Sr. Sharon and Glenda Hazel who became my new run-away friends, and, most especially to Jane Medlin who help me navigate the unfamiliar shores of the Missouri Bootheel.

Preface

In late January 2017, our daughter, Krista, announced that she was pregnant with her third child. In her next breath, she told us that she and her husband, Adrian, were moving to Tennessee with the kids. And in that moment, we decided to move to Caruthersville, MO (where Don grew up) in the extreme southeastern Bootheel (just a short 2-hour drive away), Since that day, my life has turned upside down and as I hovered on the brink of entering the seventh decade of my life, I left California to follow the grands. I hope I can find a good cup of coffee when I reach the other side.

Summer 2017

May 24, 2017 - The Road to Caruthersville, MO

We left California on May 24 and except for the occasional Facebook post from my phone, there hasn't been much heard from me. But two days ago, ATT U-Verse arrived, and I started to catch up. I knew it was only a matter of time before I would start carving out a writing space away from home. My first stop is The Roundhouse. More about this place later; now it's all about what has been going on for 20 days since May 24th.

Our travel to Missouri was blessedly uneventful. We ran into weather on our last day though we mainly were able to outrun it. We stayed for a few days in Blytheville, Arkansas, about 30 minutes south of Caruthersville, MO, while we waited for furniture to arrive. In the meanwhile, there were things to do in the house. My son Quanah and his wife Erin arrived from Indianapolis on Monday and then the heavy lifting really got started.

Our first night in Blytheville, we were under a tornado watch. According to the locals, "Welcome to the South". There was no tornado but there WAS a torrential rain that went on for hours and hours. Oh, and the mother of all thunder strikes happened, seemingly, right outside our room door. I screamed. It was like an explosion right on top of us. I learned the next morning that the intensity was so unusual, everyone in the motel lobby and the attached restaurant jumped and then became very quiet and watchful for a moment. It was that unusual.

That first night was memorable for another reason. At midnight I was wondering what in the world was going on outside in all that rain? The smoke smells and hooting and hollering were relentless. Adults. Kids. Laughter. The talk was so loud, you could follow the conversations. I finally gave up being patient at 1 a.m. and called the front desk.

Well, it seems there was to be a big family reunion the next day and this part of the family was responsible for preparing the meat. So, of course, EVERYONE had to be out there while the meat was cooking in the bar-b-ques. Sleep wasn't on their mind. I hope they had a good time the next day but, really people, haven't you ever heard of Inside Voices at 1 a.m.?

After that, it quieted down for about an hour. Just about the time I'm dozing off, it started up again. People were hooting and hollering and laughing again, as they started their trucks and cars and sped off. To deliver the meat, maybe? Anyway, if they returned, I never heard them. By 2:30, another thunderclap, like the one from hours before, would not have awoken me.

June 17, 2017 - Welcome to the South

BP, Subway, and Re-establishing My Routine

The hardest thing I've had to do since moving from California is re-establishing a writing routine. Physically, moving has been hard but emotionally, it has been a minefield.

For years I've had a variety of places to burrow into. Having writing space away from home was NOT. A. PROBLEM. When I was working, I would leave early and get an hour of writing in at House of Java. When that place changed owners and changed names, I moved on to Cafe La Mo, Crust & Crumbs, and Starbucks, but most especially my beloved Cafe La Mo, provided me a quiet, friendly atmosphere for reading, writing, and daydreaming. La Mo and Crust & Crumbs were favorite places for meeting up with friends and afterward, there was a visit to my favorite shop, Digs, or a drop in at Charity Thrift Shop. Without fail, there was something to separate me from my money and happily be carried home and added to my burgeoning collection of whatever. I have a lot of collections.

But all that has changed now. My new reality is very different. It is simpler, choices are few and what I'm used to is now far away from my new home. If I was inclined to drive 30-40 minutes to enjoy a "California" mood, I suppose I could. But making that sort of choice would blind me to the new sort of beauty that surrounds me. In a town that has more than its fair share of empty storefronts, block after block, it has, in fact many little corners of possibilities. You just must look a little harder to find them. And like all hidden gems, the unusual and unexpected, the something rare, can easily be overlooked.

So here I am, sitting inside my newly found something rare - The Subway/British Petroleum Gas Station. Oh yes, I didn't stutter- Subway/

BP, one of my new hideaways. I'm tucked into a corner, my laptop fired up and I'm feeling the words pouring out of me. Outside the window is the levee that separates the town from the Mississippi River. The soybean processing plant is nearby, and barges pull in to haul their cargo up and down the river. The Pemiscot Port Authority is maybe a mile away from the soybean plant and I have yet to discover what happens there but since this is a hardcore farming community, I'm guessing agriculture is very much involved.

Inside I am looking at a mini- grocery geared towards gasoline, drinks, and snacks. To my right is the Subway. People come and go with few sitting down. T-shirts, jeans, and work clothes are the order of the day. There isn't a hipster in sight. I must admit to a strong sense of relief about that. With the people here, what you see is what you get, and I like that a lot.

So, for now, this is my new home away from home. They have an espresso machine that turns out a good latte and the clerks double as baristas. Time for me to move on and pick up a grandé vanilla latte, hot, with a sprinkle of cinnamon for my husband Don (aka the Pirate) who is patiently waiting at home for his shot of strength.

Anne Jeffries

June 25, 2017 - Lessons on Rural Life

One of the sad lessons I've learned about living in an area with rough weather is the potential for injury to baby birds. We recently found a nest flung from a tree and yesterday we found 3 baby birds. Two were dead and one still alive. Mama was frantic. We put the bird in a box with a towel and set the box in a tree. When we came back from walking the dogs, we found the baby had flipped out of the box.

There are no nearby vets in our area and, certainly, no wildlife rescue centers. It all made me very sad and it seems like I am going to have to toughen up.

July 4th, 2017 - Midnight and Half Past Last Night

We rolled back into town very late last night. The last step in our move has been accomplished. Kris and Adrian and the littles are settled into their new home in Fairview, TN.

Waking this morning feels very strange. No cooing or gurgling sounds from Matteo. No demanding *"Mom!"* calls from Sebastian. It's so quiet, I feel like I'm in an unknown land. I have no idea what to do with myself so, since it's Independence Day, oh the irony, I think I will start with a leisurely coffee and then put on the baked beans for tonight's food and fireworks with friends.

Happy Fourth of July, my friends.
Be safe.

July 5, 2017 - On the Levee

I took my first walk along the river this morning with my daughter-in-law, Erin. It was creeping to the low 80's and humidity was already moving into the unbearable zone.

We were alone on the levee, the Bunge plant just starting to crank up business. There wasn't a tug or a barge to be seen.

Thoughts of God, new beginnings, quiet company with my daughter-in-law and, of course, a good cuppa, was a perfect start to the day. Overhead is a clouded sky offering filtered, unimposing light. Glares were absent and a hatless head merely wanted a cloth to wipe a dripping brow.

July 10, 2017 - Rolling Lightning

The rain and what it reveals to me wrote a new chapter last night. I hadn't been asleep for very long, perhaps 90 minutes at most, when we both awoke. It was around 12:20 a.m., I learned later. But in the moment of wakefulness, I could only stare, puzzled, at the window on the wall on my side of the bed. I wasn't even sure what I was looking at

Lights in varying levels of dark and bright glowed and rolled behind the blinds. Blue, black, and yellow in all their possible combinations mesmerized me for a moment. It was like a strobe light or a neon sign running out of gas, or more precisely, like the two of them happening at once putting on a light show outside my bedroom window. The worst possibility was a gathering of emergency vehicles in front of our house.

All was quiet except for the occasional distant, very distant, rumble of thunder. Finally, the sound of a driving rain penetrated my sleep-soaked brain. It was raining and what I was seeing was lightning - *big*, continuous, rolling lightning.

As I made my way to the hallway, I could see Don's darker silhouette layered against the darkness of the house. It appeared we had lost our electricity. Now I really needed to know what time it was, and I stumbled to my cell phone to turn it on and check the time. There it was: 12:20 a.m.

It was disturbing as I sat in the darkness. Despite the light show, the darkness was heavy and oppressive. I'm beginning to recognize that this might have something to do with air pressure, a variation on storms as I experienced them in California. It just didn't feel the same here.

In the light of day, the rain has passed. The heat is rising but humidity isn't pressing its terrible weight yet. My garden pots have been flung about and debris from trees, both old and new, layer our yard. A strong rake and heavy hauling to our curbside for pickup on Wednesday is in our immediate future.

Anne Jeffries

July 12, 2017 - A Truck Will Always Win

My friend Jane and I were rear ended by a semi this afternoon on the I-55 overpass between Caruthersville and Hayti. No one was hurt but we were scared witless. The semi's front bumper ended up under the car I was riding in. Slam. Spin. 180-degree turn. Thank you, guardian angels, for keeping us safe and not sending us over the side of the overpass. It would have been ugly. I am so grateful all are safe including the truck driver's dog.

I declare, between lightning strikes and semi encounters, I've screamed more times in six weeks than I've done in my entire adult life. And I don't mean yell. I mean real scream queen screaming. Think Jamie Lee Curtis and you are not far off base.

I have no idea what happened. I was totally oblivious to what was around us. Jane didn't see the semi (like they're easy to miss, you know). One moment we are moving into the left turn lane, the next, the world explodes.

I felt some tension in my muscles and took some ibuprofen when I got home. I'll take a couple more when I go to bed, but I'll be right as rain soon. Rain. Yikes. Please forgive my awful pun. Considering my new relationship with rain, that word feels weirdly wrong to me.

The morning after our encounter with an immovable object, I am feeling tip top with no lingering soreness or tension. Upon reflection, I must believe that the only reason we didn't collide against the overpass's barrier is due to the truck's bumper ending up beneath our car. Thank God for small favors.

July 17, 2017 - Rules, Not Exceptions

Since arriving in Caruthersville, I've come to learn, through disappointing experience, that getting fast food orders wrong is the rule rather than the exception. Fast food, and particularly McDonald's, was a once a week staple back home. The order rarely varied - A quarter pounder with cheese, two apple pies, and a large, hot, vanilla latte for Don and a quarter-pounder meal for me. What's to get wrong, right? I won't go into details at this point but suffice it to say that any variation beyond this simple order inevitably got mishandled. Generally, this involved items that were left out of the order. After the third time, I started scrupulously checking the contents of my bag before leaving.

I also started trying other fast food options. Since Caruthersville also has a Taco Bell, I decided to give it a try. Back home, the Taco Bell was always busy but waiting in a long line was not likely to happen here. I did remember that I liked Taco Bell, so, feeling nostalgic, I drove through the Taco Bell drive-thru and ordered the 12-taco meal, a super big something to share with Don and a side of rice and beans. And yes, I did check the bag, but this was after I was getting what felt like a bum's rush for me to get going. The long and the short of it was that the side of rice was *not* in the bag and the small item that came with the super big something was on the bottom and had been flattened. Included in the bag were enough mild taco sauce packets that I could have made a base for tortilla soup. And yes, I did open, empty, and freeze the contents. It would have been sinfully wasteful to dump all of it.

And so, went my Taco Bell experience. Once was enough. Unsurprisingly, a few months later, this Taco Bell/KFC combination location closed suddenly and unannounced. The morning shift must have been very disappointed but as I learned later, no one else was surprised. On to Sonic.

Really Sonic, how can a hamburger order go so wrong? Well, apparently, it's not hard to accomplish. Two cheeseburgers with fries, please, one with mustard and ketchup and one with mustard only. The mustard and ketchup order was fine. The mustard only - not so much since there was no mustard. There was also no tomato, lettuce, and onion either. The burger was incomplete. Hoping to hide the incompleteness, at least, from Don, I switch out my bun which had the goodies on it. But it was our mustard that graced the buns. No more Sonic for us. When service gets so bad that you are forced in the direction of not only checking the completeness of your order but also checking to make sure the burger is built right - well - enough is just flat out *enough*.

Six weeks in and the mind boggles at the sloppy dispensing of orders at three different locations by three different fast food chains. And along with the sloppiness was an attitude of service from the clerks that just couldn't be overlooked. I'm used to smiles, politeness, and friendliness. What I get is something that borders on indifference, bland disinterest, lack of animation, and in the one case, a serious case of the bum's rush. I don't get it. In an area that suffers upwards to 40% unemployment, these young people have jobs. Are service standards so low that they feel confident that their jobs are safe?

On the upside, there is also a Subway and it is a winner. Friendly clerks and food prepared correctly is a perfect prescription for many return visits. Subway has become my new go-to fast food place. As for the rest, I'm going to be better prepared with my personal grocery shopping and make my own hamburgers and fries from now on.

July 18, 2017 - Country Canning, City Sensibilities

I decide before we moved to try my hand at activities I had not done before or at least for a very, very long time. What I know about canning I can claim only from attempts done most recently in the late '80s. So basically, I'm a rank beginner.

I picked up a dozen pint jars because I didn't know where the four jars were that I *did* have since they were most likely still packed. I found a simple recipe for canning tomatoes, gathered the ingredients, and went to work. Here is what I learned.

- Sixteen vine ripe tomatoes make two jars of canned tomatoes. The third jar in the pan is mainly juice, sage, and oregano.
- It is important to have more space in a kitchen than I have in mine.
- It is essential to have the right tools to do the job most efficiently.
- It is important to buy a lot of tomatoes at the lowest price. Otherwise, you end up with 2-3 jars of very expensive tomatoes. Low yield is not a good thing.

Nevertheless, I enjoyed my experience and wouldn't mind trying it again. Next time I might make bread and butter pickles. A certain Pirate I know loves them and a well-fed Pirate is a happy Pirate. So, yo-ho-ho and off for more canning I will go. After all, I have 9 more jars to fill.

July 23, 2017 - Pecans, Peaches, and the Sound of Thunder

This quiet Sunday has been filled with early morning Mass, fellowship with friends, and after a nap, a peach/pecan pie creation. Now, punctuated by thunder heralding rain to come - maybe - it's time to talk about how I am becoming a cook.

When you live in the Bootheel of Missouri, there isn't a lot to do. There are no cinemas, bowling alleys, or nearby shopping malls. The occasional thrift store does not change often, nor does the one antique shop and what about that cute cafe for coffee and chatting over nothing in particular? Well, that's not here at all. So, women here have turned to other escapes - sewing, quilting, and cooking are, to my eyes, taking on an entirely new meaning, especially cooking.

In California, eating out was practically a way of life. Combine it with coffee with the girlfriends and thrifting, at all the ever-changing haunts and you had a recipe for reducing your pocketbook on a regular basis. But here, not so much and I find that the amazing cooks I know are drawing me into their fold.

So, what does a girl do on a quiet Sunday afternoon? Well, I have peaches from my neighbor, Miss Katherine, and I have lots of pecans from Jane. I have a ready-made Pillsbury crust and a pretty pottery dish from my dear friend, Biene, from my California life. It seemed like the time to try making a peach/pecan pie.

Never having been one for baking, I set out my bounty and thought about the advice Jane gave me over breakfast one morning. Since I have a long track record of messing up a recipe, I decided to wing it. Peaches (alas brown), pecans, and sugar were mixed in a bowl. Nothing measured but it looked right and tasted sweet enough. I sprinkled in bisquick to thicken and added in a dash of cinnamon at the end. Oh, and salt. I hoped that wasn't a last-minute bad choice.

After this, I folded the ready-made crust into my pottery dish, poured in the mixture, and topped it all with the remaining crust. I crimped the excess dough together, the aim being to seal the pie.

It wasn't pretty but I like to think it looked rustic and that is just my style.

30 minutes at 400.
Added 7 minutes and covered the crust so it wouldn't get overly brown

Taking it out, it looked perfect. After covering it with one of my vintage tea towels, it was ready for cooling, we'll see how it tastes.

The thunder is still making itself known and I'm thinking the rain will never arrive, at least not here anyway. It seems that in the space of eight short weeks I've not only started to employ my long dormant baking skills, but I have also become a storm watcher of sorts.

August 12, 2017 - That Arch

In 1924, the world was a simpler place. It was slower. There were fewer choices. Nothing makes that more evident than the presence of old highways usurped by new ones.

Living in the southeastern corner of the Bootheel makes this particularly evident. Drive 20 minutes on Hwy I-155 and you cross into Tennessee. Drive straight south on I-55 and you cross an invisible line out of Missouri and into Arkansas. A sign saying "Welcome to Arkansas" is your only clue that you have changed states.

Unlike many state line crossings, there is no monument or arch across the highway to mark this transition. However, on Old Highway 61, once the only major route between Memphis, TN, and St. Louise, MO, you will find just such an arch.

July 31st was a road trip day for Jane, Brenda, and me. It was the first time the three of us had been together again since our trip to Hall, TN in the winter of 2014. Jane wanted to introduce me to a little collection of shops, back then. It was a true destination place called "Charlene's". Today our trip was more prosaic. We ate at the Dixie Pig, waited for Jane at her medical appointment, and stopped in at the Blytheville, AR Wal-Mart.

The usual route to Blytheville is straight south on I-55, crossing that unmarked transition from one state to another. But like all rural areas, there are little bits of hidden history that, unless you are a local, or lead by a local, you will entirely miss. And so, it was that I encountered the Missouri Arch.

The Missouri Arch is a freestanding, horseshoe shaped, concrete arch that was built in 1924 by the H. H. Hall Construction Company out of Mississippi County, Arkansas. It remains the only highway arch in Arkansas to this day. In 2001 it was added to the national Registry of Historic Places and was designated part of the Great River Road. Details about the arch can be found with a simple Google search.

The Arch

Jane and Brenda both remember the arch dating back to their childhood in the 50's. They both remember getting excited when they and their siblings would see the arch because that would tell them that they were almost home. Later that evening, Don told me that Mississippi County, Arkansas was a dry county back then and just over the line, in Missouri, thirsty men could find a lot of bars and saloons. I had to smile as I imaged the weekends being especially lively.

So, now, as in 1924, I am finding that my life has become simpler, slower, and less complicated. I have one grocery store to visit. If I want a coffee drink, I go to the local BP/Subway where they have a respectable Espresso/Latte/Iced drink machine. If I need to visit a bookstore, I go to the Cape, north of me 90 minutes or I point myself southwest towards Jonesboro, Arkansas (another 90 minutes). In the meanwhile, I am intrigued by the Great River Road and am thinking about mapping out some of the "nearby" possibilities.

Anne Jeffries

August 26, 2017 - Reinventing Me Wasn't in the Plan

We've been in Missouri for three months now. I really didn't know what to expect but one thing I never would have thought of was the possibility I would find a new me. I never expected to have a new view of myself. Instead of thinking, "There is always a Plan B", my first thought these days is "There are no strangers, only people I haven't met."

After I left California, things seemed to change back there for everyone. Places weren't visited. People didn't see each other as much. Routines changed. I was saddened by this and didn't understand why but slowly I realized that the one constant in all these observations is that I wasn't there anymore. Instead of viewing myself as someone on the outside of things, I started to realize that, I was the glue that held certain things together. As I stepped back from my old life, I arrived at a clear understanding of just how I really did fit into that former life. And, I arrived at a whole new view of who I was then and who I am becoming.

Living here, I'm discovering new possibilities of what can fill my life. No one was more surprised than me when I agreed to teach second grade Sunday school. Never in my life have I *ever* wanted to work with little kids and yet here I am. And, it's fun. Someone apparently saw something in me that I didn't know was there.

I started going to city council meetings and formed relationships with a waitress and a grocery clerk. People at church were so welcoming and interested in Don and me. We felt included and part of a small but very active Catholic community. I joined the ladies' group that handles fundraising activities for various church endeavors. And in three months, there have been three big events.

Amid all this, my friend Jane really took me under her wing. Southern views and ways are not California view and ways. The way people interact with each other, how people are related to each other, the importance of the generations, going way back, and the feeling that these people are still alive and with us today is like nothing I've ever experienced before. And, of course, people talk about everybody, but seriously, I haven't heard any trash talking. People can be blunt, especially if a behavior is deemed unseemly, but people are also very forgiving and very kind. There is a connectedness here that I find very unfamiliar and Jane showed me the road map.

I've been a source of amusement to many. Lots of laughter has happened at my expense but none of it mean-spirited. Cotton. - I want to grow a plant. Sweet tea – I'm choking. Not a fan. That River - yes, the Mississippi, its sandbars, its barges, its river dykes, its *currents!* Pecans - my endless questions of how they are gathered and processed. And, explain to me the cotton picking and corn harvesting machines, and, don't forget about soybeans either. The accents - and all the forms of English I have heard since arriving here. Mice and snakes and the fact that I don't mind either, but they do have their place and that is out-of-doors. Oh, and bugs and cicadas and squirrels (tree rats to the locals). And finally, my total inability to figure out what direction I'm going. It's so relentlessly *flat* out here.

Everyone belongs to something here. First there is your church. It's just about the first thing people want to know about you. Lions Club - a free meal the first and third Thursday evening of every month. American Legion and the VFW - another free meal. Covered dish suppers at church. Tons of food and leftovers given away. *More* free food. Rotary meetings too. I don't know what night they meet but I'm sure it includes a meal.

The local library is the heart of the community. Book Club, historical society, movies on Sunday afternoon (there is no cinema in town), rental of fishing rods and bicycles, an Eclipse party, and a crew of paid staff and volunteers ready to help with whatever you need and knowledgeable in the extreme.

The thing that surprised me the most, outside of teaching catechism to second graders, of course, was my willingness to get involved in - wait for it - football. I *will* confess that I skipped the first game, but

Anne Jeffries

Don went. We won. It was 64-14 at halftime and Don walked home. A winning game was a foregone conclusion. But feeding the team brought it all to a whole different level. For one afternoon, I became a football mom!

Go Caruthersville Tigers. The football team will be here in a couple of hours. There will be lots of hungry footballers, cheerleaders, and coaches to feed before they get on the road to Maldon for their away game. C'ville has lost to Maldon 4 years in a row. We have great hopes for this year, according to those who follow these sorts of things. After all, there are twenty-two seniors on the team. That is a lot of combined experience.

By 3:30 pm, the hall had filled, and the kids ate like it was their last supper. Many of them came by before they left thanking us for the sandwich spread, shaking hands and giving the occasional hug to any of the ladies they knew well. They took all the leftovers for after the game. They are going to be a hungry group, win or lose.

And finally - there is the awesome Coach Jimmy Jackson. When we moved to Caruthersville, he recruited several young men to help move us in. He graduated from the same high school he now coaches. Big shout out to Jimmy Jackson and the terrific young men of his athletic program.

Yes, my life is very different. I find I have a greater sense of inner peace. There are friends in abundance and a solid understanding of my value that comes from the warm welcome we received. I was never a stranger, just a new someone who needed to be explored and, in a very particular Southern way, approved. Little kids like me. The community fascinates me, the lay of the land confuses me, crops and farming ways interest me, crawly and/or flying critters unhinged me but I don't mind a mouse or a snake. In fact, I wouldn't mind a snake outside for mouse control. And, football. Well, I'm going to learn all about Friday Night Lights at the next home game.

September 1, 2017 - Chicken in a Pot

A day doesn't go by when I'm either out of something or something notable happens. My life has gone from a predictable routine to a rambling road that only reveals itself when the sun rises. Of course, there are recurring moments of certainty that give shape to my week, but they are few.

- I know Sunday will bring me to church and afterward Sunday school.
- The boxes upstairs that I need to unpack are still waiting for me though their numbers grow smaller.
- There will be at least one trip to a Wal-Mart somewhere. I have three states to choose from.

But other than that, life is, thankfully, very simple and that's when things get interesting. For instance:

Monday night's meal started simply enough – a one pot chicken and vegetable dish. Cook the chicken, and then remove. Cook the veggies and then add back the chicken. So far, so good. I remove the lid, take a picture of the contents and share it back to my friend, Jane, who had sent me a picture of her dinner. Oh, and did I mention that I replaced the lid on the pan after that? Yes, indeed. And this is where it got interesting.

After nearly forty years of marital cooking, there should be few or no surprises left. But by the time dinner was served, cover still on the pan; I had stepped back into the twilight zone of Bridal Cooking. You know, ladies, all the crazy things that happen during the first year of marriage when you are getting your cooking skills together. Yeah, *that* zone. Anyway.

Anne Jeffries

The table was set. We were seated. We gave thanks for our food. I lifted the lid from the pan but, the lid didn't move. I pulled at it, tugged, twisted, tried to pry it off and handed it off to my Pirate. He can do anything. Usually.

Next stop; seek out the biggest bowl I could find. Turn the pan over - lid still on, of course. Surely the shifting weight of the contents would break it loose. I shook the pan. I banged on the pan. I ran cold water on the pan. Nothing.

Giving up, we walked away to let the contents cool off. We waited and we waited, and we waited some more. Eventually, a very hungry Pirate tried his luck again. He failed and in disgust, put the pan in the freezer, in theory for more rapid cooling with a good result. And again, we waited, and we waited. One last try was made by the irritable Pirate, and we gave up. That lid was sealed to the pan. That meal was not going to see the dark of the evening, at least not that Monday night. I decided this strange situation must have been caused by humidity. After all, this had never happened in the arid climate of California's Central Valley.

We went out in search of food and as any knowledgeable Caruthersvillian knows, that is not easily accomplished on a Monday night. However, Bros. Doug's BBQ was right around the corner and there we ended up, enjoying Butter Burgers and fries.

But the story isn't over. Yes, we were fed. And, yes, the Pirate wasn't irritable anymore. We were baffled but amused and laughed over the weird Bridal Cooking Zone moment we had stumbled into. So, feeling quite confident, he marched into the house. I continued through the kitchen, ignoring the pan on the counter, but not he. I settled onto the sofa, current book tucked into my lap and I started to read.

What followed next can only be described as an exploding pop. Seriously, I'm surprised the neighbors didn't dial 911. I ran into the kitchen convinced I would find my Pirate flat out on the floor covered in our erstwhile meal. But no. There he stood, looking at the pot, the lid still stubbornly sealed to it. However, it had changed. Apparently, he had pried it loose just enough to break the seal, releasing all the trapped air. That event also destroyed my lid. It wasn't pretty.

The Lid Collage

This time he managed to separate the lid from the pan and there was our meal, safe and ready for consuming. I looked at my Pirate and grinning, said, "Well, I guess I won't have to make dinner tomorrow."

September 5, 2017 - That Painting!

I visited Chandler's Furniture in Dyersburg, TN, recently and as I entered the showroom, I was brought to a standstill by the painting hanging on the entrance wall. Not only could you not miss it, it would not be ignored. I don't know if this post would have been written if Harry Hart had not been at the door, but he was and there was the beginning of my next post for "Tales from the Bootheel".

Yes, I know. Dyersburg isn't precisely part of the Bootheel but when your own small town has lost its small Wal-Mart which wasn't a Superstore like the surrounding big boys, well, even an itty-bitty Wal-Mart can't compete. So, consequently, we C'ville folks cross the river a lot. Memphis has its West Memphis in Arkansas. We have (or at least I have) an East Bootheel. I'm in Tennessee a lot and so it was that this day I was in Chandler's and Mr. Hart told me the story of the remarkable and very big painting.

It was an Easter morning service at the Dyersburg First Church of Christ. As the pastor preached, a lady of the church community commenced painting an amazing portrait of Christ, all with her hands, not a brush in sight, behind the pastor. By the time the service was over the painting was completed. Harry Hart was so moved by the power of the painting that he eventually asked if it could be moved to Chandler's where it could be viewed by anyone who entered the store and could be seen from the road, as well.

As I viewed the painting, I continued to visit with Harry as he proudly spoke of the young and vibrant church community that had grown from a membership of 400 to over 3,500 souls now. Along with this remarkable painting, there seemed to also be an openness to all in the town and various church communities. Each Sunday at each service

2 or 3 of the other local churches, their congregations, and the pastor are specifically prayed for by name.

Coming from radically liberal California, one of the things that has most impressed me is the importance of church here. It is practically the first thing people want to know about you. The lessons of Christ are taken seriously here. People of faith take it seriously in California, as well, but unlike California, where faith is disdained by the powers that be, or the moneyed, or alt-lifestyle folks, not to mention the influential entertainment industry, in Missouri, there is a balance, an inclusiveness, a desire to serve all that does not exist in California anymore. Granted, Missouri's not perfect, but there is a whole lot more thoughtfulness and care brought to the political table here and that painting, so boldly displayed in a Tennessee town, drove the point home.

Where there are people, there will always be problems but, where there is Christ and/or a strong belief in a good and loving God, there is a path to sane living and I'm seeing a lot of it here. And, *that* gives me hope,

September 11, 2017 - Let's Talk About Café Culture

A few years ago, the Pirate and I spent a winter in Caruthersville, Missouri, specifically; it was January through March 2014. It was cold that year, a hard one, and shocking to me to whom wet, icy winters were an unknown. I didn't get to know C'ville well that winter; we were there to work with Glenmary Sister, Sr. Darlene Presley, assisting with her mission work which was, and still is, spread across the whole of Pemiscot county. Fast-forward to June 2017 and the Pirate and I have settled here permanently. I knew going into this move that life would change radically for me. The cafe culture of my small valley town would be a complete unknown in my new world. Or, at least I thought it would be.

Around the world, the idea of a social atmosphere surrounding the consumption of coffee is common. These social centers became a hub for artists, intellectuals, writers, and people who just like to talk and solve the problems of the world. You can hear interesting and unexpected snippets of conversation and you look around and discover a circle of mature men, talking about who knows what but clearly Lord Byron or Wellington is involved. Not to mention further discussions about the destruction of history and going out and ringing some tail. Truth be told, I'd be ringing some tail with them. It *is* our history and hiding it or destroying it isn't going to change it. Anyway, back to cafe culture.

Back home, we had a solid, deeply entrenched café culture. For ten blocks, my small town had coffee shops, cafes, restaurants, thrift shops, antique shops, art galleries, spas, museums, and boutiques. A whole seasonal series of events grew up around this ten-block area - Christmas Parade, 4th of July, and Halloween all with the requisite vendors with everything from handmade goods to China imports. And, of course, there was always a car show at one end of these multi-block extravaganzas. Thursday evenings and Saturday mornings brought out the farmers' markets. Oh, the luscious produce and deliciously crafted olive oils, salsas, BBQ sauces - makes my mouth water even now.

As my time extended here and drew itself out, I found that, with patience, I could find small, isolated pockets of my past. I recently discovered Riverside Stationers, Trinkets and Treasures, and the Crow's Nest. I've spotted two other places on Truman Boulevard that are exploration worthy and I'll get there soon. The only downside to the places I've discovered is that they are all so spread out, so disconnected from each other. These five places together, in one area, could become a magnet for other small businesses and I've had the pleasure of talking to at least two other women who share my daydream and, dare I say, vision. Add to that C'ville's fabulous river front access and you have a prescription for revitalization. And, you know, it doesn't have to be high end. There can be something for everyone. I noticed a wide range of prices on the gift goods at Riverside Stationers. The possibilities are endless.

So, what is *my* dream? Well, whether I create it or someone else does, what is better than a place offering coffee and conversation and books? How about a place that regularly features local artists? There are a lot of gifted people we don't necessarily know about except by word of mouth. How about the Cookie Lady? And just yesterday I learned about a woman who apparently makes to-die-for cinnamon rolls and other sweets. There really is a lot of beauty in the Bootheel. Unlike its more obvious sisters in other places, you just have to look for it a little harder here.

Anne Jeffries

September 15, 2017 - There Are No Strangers

Have you ever felt like you were not a part of something; that the world surrounding you, whether neighborhood or larger community, was an unknown and you yourself an unknown? Well, welcome to my world. Growing up a Navy brat, we moved a lot and even though we settled in San Diego in 1961, the moving around years marked me as always feeling like an outsider. Then as an adult moving around in California, that feeling continued. When you come from a place but move around a lot within it, you find you have no history to bring to the table that anyone else might relate to.

Fortunately, my kids didn't grow up that way. They were surrounded by an uncle and grandparents and a stable school and church community. There is a lot to be said for roots, for building history in a place, for leaving but always returning or, never leaving at all. I didn't understand the attractions of living in a small world until I moved here. And by moving here, I discovered, at the tender age of pushing 70, that I had found a place I could call home. No one could have been more surprised than me.

I have precious memories of my life in California, mainly wrapped up in my love for a few good friends that while now distant, are still close and dear to me. I arrived here anxious and not a little fearful. The people and touchstones that gave my life form and shape were clearly going to be missing and I had absolutely no history attached to this place; I only had a series of well-spaced visits of short duration. But it was here that I discovered that there are no strangers. Back in my California life, people didn't talk easily to each other outside of their own group. People, in general, were superficially friendly and guarded. If you smiled at someone, that's all you did. Then you quickly looked away.

And then I landed here, in this small town that felt like the end of the earth and the dominant feeling I felt almost immediately was a feeling of acceptance. People were curious about us. What were we doing here, of all places? My Pirate was easily explained. He had come home, but, what about me? I heard a lot of folks saying, "You must really be feeling culture shock." Well, yes, I really was feeling it. But then, almost like magic, within three months I felt happy and genuinely content. I wasn't a stranger and I was genuinely interested in everyone I met. I wanted to discover who they were and be ready to remember them the next time I saw them and believe me, in a small town, you always see someone again. So suddenly I found that the smile that hid quickly in California was here followed up by a hello and sooner or later, an introduction. I found myself so comfortable talking with complete strangers that a kind of hyper-awareness enveloped me. I found myself talking to people everywhere.

This week I'm in Fairview, Tennessee outside of Nashville. Our daughter just had her third child and first girl. We are very happy, but it was in this setting that I expanded my potential for connecting with people. Nashville is no small town, but I met a frightened and very pregnant woman at the hospital, and she was alone. I was able to sit with her for a while and distract her from her anxiety until she could finally connect with her family. And today I met a young military woman, full-time Army National Guard. We were waiting for food to go and I'm never one to ignore a uniform, so we got to talking. Lord, I'm sure glad we did. She and my husband shared the same Military Occupation Specialty otherwise known as MOS. She was Active Guard Reserve like him, and most surprisingly, they were in the same sort of unit, drug interdiction. You could have knocked me over with a feather. Of course, she would have never volunteered that information, but I mentioned his work and that opened another door.

I'm convinced, now in my golden years, that there really are no strangers and I am determined to meet as many people as possible. There is nothing to fear from people. Yes, there are fearsome people; a lot of them. But I prefer to see them as human beings who, like everyone else, just need a smile and a hello.

Autumn

September 26, 2017 - Let's Talk About Cotton

Arriving here in the Bootheel, in late May, I had big ideas about growing a cotton plant. To the surprise of no one, this notion was met with a lot of laughter and not a few scoffs, not to mention downright derision. This only served to increase my determination. It also got me to thinking about where and when this idea was birthed, so now, well into the 21st century and in the midst of a derangement I call the Politics of Cotton, I can only reflect upon how innocent this plant is in our ongoing and sometimes bloody discourse on racism.

Back home, cotton was on my back; never on my personal radar. Sometime in the last quarter of the 20th century, I was on one of my brief and widely spaced visits to Caruthersville. Pirate pointed out a lone cotton plant that was well into its maturity and he plucked a boll and presented it to me. I still have that soft, white bit of fluff. Three or four years ago I plucked a friend for it from a landscaping plant outside of the New Madrid Museum. It was February 2014 and a few brave little plants stood up to the below freezing weather, their beds as white as the bolls that still adorned them. Now I had two Bootheel bolls.

Along the way, I have heard family stories, some going back generations, of growing cotton. It was hard, dirty, and painful work at harvest time. In the extreme heat, farm owners, sharecroppers, and laborers were all out in the fields picking, bagging, sweating, and toiling together. And, in that heat, they shared the same water from the same barrel. Only one thing mattered; bringing in the crop.

These bits of lore fascinated me and inspired me so, not unexpectedly, I wanted to be a part of this story. It seemed like an ideal way to fit in and identify with the entire community. In one way or another back here, everyone has a story about cotton. Even my Pirate has stories about the field behind his house.

Once people knew I was deadly serious about growing a cotton plant, they sort of got on board with the idea. They were still reserved about the chances of my success since they were growers on a large scale. I think it was hard for them to focus on the possibility and potential of my small-scale vision. But they did get on board.

Christina, our local newspaper editor, is going to get me into a harvester. I've been warned of dirt, dust, and spiders. Does anyone have a hazmat suit I can borrow? Shout out to our two chiefs -Fire and Police - both men named Jones, no relation. The Jean and Ladeen twins will help me gather up good dirt from a field come planting time, and Farmer Danny (you know who you are) promised me a cotton stalk. In truth, what I got was a yanked up entire plant thanks to a midnight run on a field somewhere. He's going to show me how to harvest and store the seeds. Later, there will be planting and cultivation lessons. Bless his heart. Online reading will fill in the details. I plan to get the Pirate into this, too. He has a good eye and I know he will pick out the best planting location. I hope it's out front. I would love sharing my growing adventures with my neighbors.

You know that old ad line? Cotton is the fabric of our lives? Well, it's true and it does have its messy moments just like life. Life isn't perfect just as cotton's story isn't perfect, but we've all benefited from it and the lessons it has been able to teach us.

October 1, 2017 - Music in the Bootheel

Sadly, music unraveled in my life as the family grew up and went in different directions. Our circle of friends didn't celebrate music as my father did. From time to time we would enjoy a group playing at a local cafe on a summer night, but I found I didn't really connect with much of what I heard. And if I didn't connect with it, I'm sure it was an exercise in love and patience for my Pirate because he didn't enjoy a young music scene. But suddenly I find it all changing. There is a bit of a music scene in Caruthersville.

Saturday evening found me in the cozy home of Joy McGraw, joined by her sister Jane Rodgers and her husband, Dennis. The Pirate had been sick all week and all I can say is, boy, did he miss out. I connected and he would have loved it. For starters, there wasn't an amp in sight. Two guitars, one mandolin, and several harmonicas produced an evening of beautiful music. Joy's lovely voice harmonized with Dustin Walters. Jerry Lintner's guitar filled out the sound and Bill from Blytheville added a sound of aching longing to the strains as they played out. Bluegrass flowed into old southern gospel, Proud Mary and the Beatles and the Turtles followed in quick succession and back again to blue grass. By the time I left, we had all enjoyed an old highland ditty about a Scotsman and his kilt. The ladies tittered with laughter.

I was walked home by two new friends and was ready for more. The local radio station plays a lot of old school country music and, unexpectedly, I love it. I hear there is music at Little Pizza Heaven on some weekends and it's guaranteed acoustic, no amps and no drums. Shout out to Mike and Jean. That will make my Pirate very happy. And best of all, music has wound its way back into my life again. My dad is no doubt very happily listening in and tapping a toe.

October 8, 2017 - What I've Learned About Mice

Before moving here, mice were not part of my reality. Up until now, I can probably count the number of mice I've seen, outside of a lab, on two hands and not use all my fingers. My mother's house in a rural town in Southern California in the mid-1970's was my first encounter. She hated mice. I thought they were cute. It wasn't until decades later that I was introduced to rats, specifically, the urban loving Norway rat. I. Do. Not. Like. Rats.

Rats like to live in groups. They like to breed. They will eat and drink anything. They are bold with a capital B. Nothing scares them. Their ability to move through their environment is phenomenal. They will chew through just about anything and they have the nasty habit of appearing in unexpected places like, in my gardening pots in my garden shed back in California. But that is a story I won't inflict on you.

However, I can proudly say that my Pirate is very brave and battled them back and then cleaned out the shed and secured it against future invasions. I also can happily say that my son-in-law is no slouch in the rat fighting department either. His efforts broke the dam that swept the nasty critters away setting the stage for the big clean-up and re-enforcement against future invasions. So, whilst my experience with mice is minimal, I am well acquainted with rats. Then I moved to Caruthersville.

Buying a house, sight unseen, except for lots of pictures online, and most especially a house that is seventy-two years old, will no doubt come with a few surprises. But the joy of getting this house on *this* street in Caruthersville was a true childhood dream come true for the Pirate and, for me that simply made all the surprises merely interesting challenges. So far, we've been checking things off our fix-it list one item at a time. When a house is so old you need to have a lot of patience and simply take the long view on getting things done. Yet, there was one battle I had not expected. While the house was well maintained and bug and spider free, it had sat empty for a while and this made it an irresistible lure for mice. Lots and lots of mice. Oh, my word, so many mice.

Unlike most if not all the people I've met since arriving here, I was completely clueless about mice and their habits. I would soon learn. Mice are nocturnal. They don't like bright lights. They are shy and prefer to hide. Amongst themselves, they are very social. And like rats, they breed and eat anything and everything. And what they're not eating, they're chewing up to create nesting material. The thing about mice is that they are so charmingly cute. They're Disney cute and I've never been bothered by them. They find specific hangouts and stick to their routines and routes. If it was just one, I probably wouldn't be too bothered. The thing is, they don't remain at just one. So, our mouse hunt was on.

The Pirate and St. Francis of Assisi would have been great friends but even the harmless Pirate understood that mice don't belong in a house, so he successfully ousted at least two separate raiding parties in the 4 months we've been here. The mouse kill has been substantial, but he does have his limits. Whenever a mouse was merely caught, usually by a foot or tail, he would gently carry it away from the house and release it, thereby allowing nature to take its course. I'm guessing that one of those courses led right back to our house.

People in the know about this suggested, and rightly so, that he might as well hang out a welcome sign. I just sit back and shake my head. I figure if he's doing the heavy lifting of making our house a mousy killing field, who am I to critique the methodology? And speaking of methodology, the other thing I learned about mice is that they can't chew through steel wool. After verifying this with a few locals who have had their own battles with mice, the Pirate went to work scouting out holes and cracks in an effort to keep the little critters out. And, while I trust he has found most, if not all, access points, have I mentioned that I also don't mind snakes? I wouldn't mind have a gopher snake making a cozy home around our foundation

October 20, 2017 - Let's Talk About Food

California feeds the country. No one would argue that. And having so much fresh produce available is an irresistible lure to aspiring chefs, chefs who have arrived, and foodies everywhere. The variety of food styles in California is without a doubt one reason why a person might even stay there. If you are looking for ethnic, organic, vegetarian, vegan, or fresh from the ocean fish, you won't have to travel far. For a dedicated Foodie, there is absolutely no place like California for originality and variety and potential for creating the next food trend. And, the food is *good*. Marry food creativity to beer, coffee, and wine crafting, as well as small presses of pure, unblended olive oils and you have the perfect accompaniment to the rich and varied foods of California. Aside from a few treasured friends, food is probably number one on my list of things I miss the most about California.

And did I forget to mention food trucks? What was once a Mexican food monopoly has spread into a wonderland of food fare that is at its absolute *best* because it comes from a truck. Standing on the street eating whatever delectable choice has fallen into your hands raises the hotdog or pretzel from a cart to a whole new level. Coffee trucks, curry cuisine, corn dogs, empanadas, grilled cheese, kababs, Chinese, BBQ, shrimp and lobster, desserts and donuts and cinnamon rolls, or waffles with anything and everything available to top it off, it is all there. A road trip through California is foodie heaven.

I've driven across the country many times over my 70 years and one thing I've noticed repeatedly is that food outside of CA is mainly, well, boring. Sure, there are pockets of fabulous and regional foods can leave a person crying for more, but mainly food is unimaginative. One of my worst memories was ordering a salad and receiving a wedge of iceberg covered with a dollop of mayonnaise. It was just terrible. I happen to love wedge salads dripping with blue cheese dressing, heavy with chunks of blue cheese and bacon. That's the gold standard for me. On the other hand, the absolute best biscuits I ever had were from a local diner somewhere in northern Texas right off Interstate 40. There was a hotel, a gas station, the diner, and a tractor/farm equipment repair shop. That was it and all surrounded by 1000's of acres of farmland. Those biscuits just about made me cry. The waitress sent us off with a bag full of warm deliciousness for the road.

Anyway, I come by my food opinions honestly. Between a lifetime of California freshness and creativity to a fair amount of travel, I've earned my stripes as a food snob. So, when I arrived in the Bootheel, I wasn't surprised to learn I would have to do some serious digging to find food that made my heart sing.

My first discovery was that not all barbecues are made equal. It also became very clear to me why HGTV loves to show barbecue food war shows. People are passionate about their barbecue in the South and Midwest. Oddly enough, I discovered that I was too, something I didn't know until I landed in the Bootheel. To say that BBQ here is different from California BBQ is like saying that Notre Dame Cathedral is different from a chapel. My friend, Jane, will testify to my barbecue snobbery. But I've learned that I'm in good company. Everyone has an opinion about barbecue.

No one would argue that there are endless choices for barbecue in the Bootheel. Dixie Pig, Chubby's, Cole Mama's, and Brother Doug's, are just four of the places I've tried. Each is good and each is very different from the other. But it was Brother Doug's barbecue that sang "Home!" Succulent, red, and shredded, it set off a party in my mouth. My ideal barbecue is pork, shredded and dripping with a dark red/brown sweetish sauce. No tart vinegar flavor allowed. It was at Chubby's where I finally got the idea of mixing the skinny vinegar-based sauce that's called BBQ sauce around here, with ketchup. It was pure heaven and the tartness was subjugated.

Patty Ann's has good salads. Little Pizza Heaven wins the local pizza wars. There is nothing like a pizza that shouts, "Just like my mom's". And Bros. Doug's makes a darn good burger. Daylight Donuts wins for best homemade potato chips. Who knew homemade chips would be a thing? I love homemade chips, something not commonly found in my part of California.

Something else not usually found back home is deep fried chicken livers. Once we hit Oklahoma, I started noticing fried chicken livers on every menu we perused. I tried them all. Lamberts even got a couple of tries, as did Patty Ann's. I was surprised to discover that good as all the various livers were, the standout place, without a doubt, is the Roundhouse in Caruthersville. Now here is good, old-fashion eating at its finest. Unpretentious, stuck in time, friendly, and comforting, Roundhouse fits like a beloved old slipper. I love going there. They set the standard for, not only the yumminess of their livers, but they are super-friendly, always remember your name even when you are a newbie, and my tea is always unsweet, God Bless them.

Like everything else, since arriving here, I'm enjoying the simplicity of life, the simplicity of living in of a town with few choices. The restaurants and cafes are mainly mom and pop, serve good comfort food and a juicy burger. They may keep odd hours but that works too. People head across the river to Dyersburg, Tennessee, or to the Cape, Kennett and, even Jonesboro, Arkansas, on the weekends for big shopping and generally end up eating there, too. Anyway, those down times have helped me organize myself so that instead of going somewhere in town, I'm at home, doing what I love best - writing and continuing the re-invention of my new life.

November 6, 2017 - Dream Large

Christmas was always special to the Pirate and more so because he had so little - no siblings, nothing to really call his own, an unstable sense of place because of the moving back and forth between the small town and two much larger cities. At Christmas time, the street he walked along to school was like a fairytale. To his young eyes, these were grand homes, with bright, twinkling windows, and welcoming porches. Front yards were adorned with almost life-size mangers. None of this was at home so walking to school, on this street was like walking through a wonderland. His dream took form and at last, he could put it into words. "Someday I would like to own a house on this street."

Fast-forward almost sixty years and most of his life is behind him. Two children. Three grandchildren. A long marriage. It has been a challenging life but a good life. The daydream was long behind him but not forgotten. The older he grew the more clearly, he saw the possibility of a life on that street. But, one of the things you learn in adulthood is that sacrifices must be made and if the choice is between an old dream and nearness to family, well, the family will win every time. Unless something changed. And change, it did.

And so, with that change, he found himself deep within that early sigh on his heart and surrounded by a dream unfolding, a dream coming true. That street, that house, reconnection with old friends - it was all coming to life, an unexpected life. He has never been happier.

Dedicated to my Pirate

November 13, 2017 - Language in the Flatlands

The two summers before moving to the Bootheel, Pirate and I taught English as a Second Language (ESL) in a migrant farm camp not far from where we lived. We had minimal Spanish, so we relied heavily on teaching the basics of pronunciation, conversation, and language structure. Many of the families came from Mexico or arrived from other encampments in Texas and Arizona. Those who lived at the camp were all documented and the camp itself was a mission through the Migrant Worker Program of the Catholic Diocese of Stockton. Sr. Edith, from Mexico, managed the day to day matters of the people, seeing to their spiritual and personal concerns. Like many nuns, she had a way of asking for something and you just could not say *no*. And so, it was that we learned the intimacy of communicating without a common language. By our third summer we were on the road out of California and interestingly, Sr. Edith was transferred to Eutah, Alabama, just a short 5-6-hour drive from us. I expect we will be seeing Sr. Edith again, sooner rather than later.

Language, and more specifically, how language sounds, has always appealed to me. Like interesting faces that capture my attention, so does the sound of the human voice. It's no surprise to me that landing in the Bootheel has set off a party in my ears.

The first thing I learned is that not all Bootheelers sound like my Pirate. After 50 plus years away from here, his drawl has softened to the sound of a slow-moving creek over a bed of rounded stones. The second thing I learned is that you can't associate one accent with the Bootheel. The voices here have moved up from Arkansas, Alabama, and Mississippi, over from Tennessee, and down from northern Missouri, which sounds very different from southern Missouri. Even Kentucky and West Virginia are represented. We have Katrina, most recently, to thank for Louisiana's presence.

Locals continue to be amused as I trek through the ocean of sounds and usually all it takes is a *what?* from me and a puzzled look. That's when I get the *right* pronunciation and a spelling lesson. Most recently, my GPS and I discovered there is no such place as Hawkem. I was looking for a place called Strawberries, which by unanimous agreement, has the best barbecue in the Bootheel. Believe me; unanimous doesn't come easy when it comes to BBQ in the Heel so this place must be something. My snooty California BBQ self will have to check this out. Anyway, I was finally steered in the right direction when I learned that Hawkem was really *Holcomb*. Who knew an "L" would be silent and an "om" would sound like an "em"? What I call my Standard English had taken yet another hit.

The most remarkable example I can give of this sound trick is from three years ago when we were on an extended visit and the Wal-Mart was still opened. Anyone who lives here knows that Caruthersville is small enough that on shopping day you can encounter the same person at several different places. So, when I arrived at the Hays Market after leaving Wal-Mart, I was struck by seeing a really fascinating looking man whom I had first seen at the checkout line in Wal-Mart. Now he was at the meat counter in Hays. Well, as I've said before, there are no strangers and three years ago it was just as true. He was short and strong looking as a fireplug and dark as a moonless night in the desert. And he was just as friendly then as he was earlier, chatting people up who were also in line. So, I said hello and nice to see you again so soon or some such friendly thing like that. But this time I got the full-on blast of his voice, his accent. The man was speaking English, but I didn't understand a single word he said. My ears and attention homed in on his voice and after a few minutes of friendly chatter, I came away feeling like I had encountered an unusual English/Cajun/Creole dialect, Gullah. I had seen a few videos from my linguistics studies days in college and of course, now YouTube is a treasure chest of languages to listen to. I sure would like to see that man again.

Another area I got hung up on initially was how to pronounce certain town names. Blytheville isn't pronounced "Blithe" ville? Why does the "Ma" of Madrid have a short "a" sound instead of the softer "ah" sound and why is Madrid pronounced with an emphasis on the first syllable? Fill this all up with colorful phases and some of the nicest insults I've ever heard, bless his heart, and you have a recipe for some fun listening time.

I used to tease the Pirate at the ESL classes when I would tell the students that he spoke a form of English and not to listen to how he pronounced words. All his i's and e's sound the same. I spoke Standard English and with proper pronunciation. But the joke is on me. Listening to the lively sounds of language here, well my California Standard English really does sound rather boring. I need to start learning some Southern.

November 20, 2017 - What I've Learned About Farming and Ginning

Since moving to Missouri, I've been surrounded by birds, birds, and more birds. The Cardinals aren't around too much yet. Perhaps they will arrive when it is colder. But robins and jays abound. Yesterday, geese were flying overhead, moving farther south. I heard an owl last night and today a hawk soared across the front window of my car. And, who can miss the sound of a woodpecker?

I've also noticed a lamentable absence of cattle, something that was so common in my former world. Not only were dairy farms in abundance, there were herds of beef cattle, sheep, and horses. Farmers grew hay, corn, and alfalfa. In the orchards, there were olives, peaches, and almonds. On the edges of our town, there were large, open areas called Green Belts kept between small towns to inhibit housing and strip mall development. There was always something growing there or grazing there.

But here, like there, farming doesn't bear much resemblance to my Charlotte's Web vision of farming. You know *Charlotte's Web*, that lovely children's book of farm life and saving the life of one runty little pig. This endearing story, like the song *Old MacDonald Had a Farm*, laid out the classic vision of farm life. But is it like that here? No, not so much.

One of the things I have learned is that a farmer doesn't necessarily live on his farm. He has acreage. He might be growing all over the area cobbling together a farming life that might have once been counted in the 1000's of acres, now reduced by time, fewer children taking up the family business, and worse, taxes. The family farm has or had a home and barn or maybe a big shed for large equipment, but chickens aren't running around, kitchen gardens, if there, aren't visible, and the closest farmers market is 40 minutes away and is a relatively small affair.

Replacing this time-honored vision are cotton pickers, harvesters, and combines. Trucks haul the harvest to granaries and gins there to be processed and hauled by truck or barge to elsewhere. I decided early in my life here that I would not only grow a cotton plant of my very own, *but*, when teased with the idea, I would ride in a cotton picker and visit a cotton gin. Both of those things happened a few weeks ago.

Visiting a gin was an event unlike anything I have ever experienced. There is a hum and whir in the air that never quiets. Cotton bricks are dropped and processed; fiber and seeds are separated from the brick and sent off to pour into another machine where fiber and seed are separated, fiber going in one direction and seed in the other.

The separated fiber eventually is reassembled into smaller bales, shipped to a storage area where brokers sell the bales that move out to parts unknown all over the world. Here's a piece of trivia for you.

One bale of cotton can make:

215 Jeans
249 Bed Sheets
409 Men's Sport Shirts
690 Terry Bath Towels
765 Men's Dress Shirts
1,217 Men's T-Shirts
1,256 Pillowcases
2,104 Boxer Shorts
2,419 Men's Briefs
3,085 Diapers
4,321 Mid-Calf Socks
6,436 Women's Knit Briefs
21,960 Women's Handkerchiefs
313,600 $100 Bills

And what about the separated seed? Cottonseed is used in the making of cooking oil or in salad dressings. It is also used in the production of shortening and margarine. Cotton grown for the extraction of cottonseed oil is one of the major crops grown around the world to produce oil, after soy, corn, and canola oil. It is also useful as a cosmetic ingredient commonly found in lipstick, mascara, and lip balms

By far the most exciting time of the day, though, was me climbing up into the cotton picker. I thank God, every time I think of it, that no one had a camera except me, of course, and I was firmly in possession of it. The vision of me climbing up that ladder to the platform that held the cab would not have been a pretty one. But, once settled in next to Mr. Sides, I had the time of my life.

The climb down from the picker was much more easily accomplished. It's amazing how, when you work *with* gravity, things go much smoother.

And another experience is under my belt and I've gained new insight into the ways of farming, imagined and real, and cotton's product after being picked. Now if I can just get a ride on a barge. Or is it the push tug I'd like to ride on? Are there any offers out there for me?

Winter/Spring 2018

January 1, 2018 - Driftwood, Then and Now

Certain things go hand in hand when I reflect on my California memories. Two of the most prominent are driftwood and fog. Growing up in San Diego, the fog was as normal as breathing. There is a mysterious whisper in the air and sounds travel great distances. Conversations can be overheard leaving no sense of direction as to where the hushed murmurs are arising from. The warning sound of a foghorn sighs mournfully, casting out a repeated signal on the fog washed beaches of my memories.

Countless times, I walked on a fog-embraced beach, fog so thick; it was gray and sunless at noon. My only company a few other fog walking devotees, driftwood, seashells, and the remains of giant kelp. Driftwood was something I viewed as in endless supply. Picking it up, feeling it, smelling it, returning it, was all part of the beach walking ritual. Back then it never occurred to me to keep it. Once I moved away from the ocean, I became acquainted with fog's valley cousin but unlike the seashore, the valley fog had no driftwood. I began to discover what I had missed. And then, on another foggy day, next to a different body of water, I rediscovered driftwood.

Like the Pacific Ocean, the Mississippi River has a lively and unpredictable life. Good weather shows running currents and occasional floating debris. Like the ocean, much of the debris is hidden underwater. But, unlike the ocean, its currents run very visibly, like rivers within rivers, breaking up a multitude of fragments, great and small, that have broken from some birthing place and have been formed into something unrecognizable. River driftwood had washed up at my feet, on a completely unexpected shore.

The end of Ward Avenue has a boat ramp and I'll occasionally walk to the bottom of the ramp and dip my toes into the river. In the heat of summer, sandals dipped into the river make for a much more satisfying experience but winter's cold discourages such indulgence on bare feet. What it doesn't have in short supply, for the moment, is driftwood that has been thrown up high upon the boat ramp's rocky embankment.

Like softly finished gems thrown upon the river shore, trunks, limbs, branches, and fragments just lay there waiting for me. I felt ambushed. The Pirate, meanwhile, waited for me in the car with no idea of what awaited him. As I happily arrived with four bits and pieces, he opened the back door of the car, smiled at me knowingly, and took my treasures off to their new home.

Driftwood

I'm already mentally weaving a wall hanging for one and seascapes of tiny houses, boats, and cliffs are evolving for the others. And, the Pirate has already acknowledged that come spring he will be there holding a box while I load up with winter's bounty that is next delivered to my riverfront door.

January 8, 2018 - Baby, It's Cold Outside

Coming from the California valley, we get our fair share of cold weather. I've lost plants in the brief freeze periods that visited us during December and January. It wasn't unusual to see all my succulents protected by dome-shaped covers, sheets, and towels to save them from a frosty death. Orchards and vineyards are dotted with smudge pots in the relentless battle to save fruit, nut, and olive bearing trees, as well as grape vines, from a killing frost that could devastate fragile blossoms and emerging fruits. If you have noticed fluctuating costs in your fruits, over the years, you can chalk it up to a killing frost and a battle lost in a bad winter.

Winter was also a period when I would make small alterations to my clothing habit. Going out in the low to mid 40's with just a light jacket or a blanket shawl was usually enough for me to feel comfortable. The sandals changed to shoes but no socks. If it rained, there was the umbrella, hooded rain jacket optional. Shoes were a concession to not slipping on rain wet surfaces. Granted I was a bit extreme. Other, less hearty individuals, layered up, pulled on socks and wore gloves. My son was worse than I was. Sandals were basically year-round. His first winter in graduate school, in Ohio didn't faze him. Sandals were the foot covering of choice fall, winter, and spring. Even I thought that was a little crazy. Of course, that can be chalked up to youth. Later, years of living in Oregon and then Indiana taught him the virtue of shoes, socks, layering, hats, coats, and gloves. These are lessons I still am learning.

Learning these lessons haven't been easy; first I had to figure out why 32 degrees in California didn't feel like 32 degrees here. Thirty-two degrees is *cold*, down to the bone and stiffen up the knees cold. So why? A temperature is a temperature, right? Well, no, not really. First off, cold in California is dry. The relatively low humidity of cold air in my old home meant that conduction of heat off a body was slower. A body retains heat longer. High humidity and low temperatures, on the other hand, create bone-chilling cold.

Socks soon became a staple in my wardrobe. Gloves now stay in my purse. They don't get set aside. They *do not* get lost. Two scarves are used when one would have been just fine in past winters. And layering is necessary. Repeat that. *Necessary.*

The thing about weather is that it's not just cold, damp winters. It's also high humidity springs and summers. That requires clothing combat of a different sort. Apparently, the mosquitoes in California didn't like me. I never got bit. However, their Missouri cousins like me just fine. In fact, I am very tasty considering the bites I encountered my first summer here. The worst of it was the bites on my feet. I've already decided that socks and semi-enclosed shoes will be my new footwear. And I really don't care how hot and humid it is. The pants will be long. The t-shirts will have long sleeves, and most importantly, I will be covered, head to toe, in DEET.

January 14, 2018 - In the Gray Time

It has been hard to concentrate recently, much less focus on anything. Three weeks of family illness, my immobilization from a knee injury, a heavy dose of homesickness, and winter's gloom have all contributed to a feeling of malaise that is hard to shake. After a while, you feel like river fog has wrapped itself around you, blocking out the light of day.

When I was prepping for snow and ice, I wished there was some sort of checklist for stocking food. I'm sure there is such a list somewhere on Google, but pain and discomfort kept me off my laptop during the time when the planning and prepping should have been happening.

One important question that needs answering is what do you do if you lose power and you have an all-electric kitchen? I think I have a Coleman camp stove around somewhere in the garage, but do I have propane? Worse yet, if I do have propane, does the stove even work? It has been literally decades since it's been used. I suppose, at a minimum, it needs a good cleaning.

So, there is a lot I don't know about and literally, have no idea what to do. Friends have been excellent sources of information and guidance but there's just nothing that can prepare you for the feeling of icy, hard-packed snow beneath your feet and especially when you are just beginning to feel steady on your feet again.

Except for Thursday's medical appointment, today is the first day I've been out in a week. Today I learned what salt looks like on the church steps. Friends Nancy and Byron kindly picked me up for Mass. I am most definitely going to need driving lessons for navigating snowy roads. It was cheering to be around people again and the church was warm and snug. It felt like God was giving me a hug. Coffee afterward added to the uplifted feelings. I am convinced that cabin fever is one part being stuck inside and three parts missing the companionship of friends.

Adding to my total lack of preparedness, I knew I was running low on things in the kitchen. It never occurred to me to ask for help but apparently, that is what people think of first around here. So, thank you, Byron and Nancy, for thinking for me and offering to take me to Hays before taking me home. The cupboard isn't quite so bare now.

When I had convinced myself that I would have nothing to say this week, the cobwebs miraculously cleared. The fog lifted and I saw my way to gratitude for the friends who help so generously. But now it has started snowing again. I suppose there will be a couple more months of this to look forward to. The next time I'm out, I'll do better at stocking up.

January 22, 2018 - The River

When we moved here, I knew I would be leaving behind a lot that I loved and thrived on. If I could choose one word to describe my old world, that word would be "access." I lived in a small-size city of 70,000 that, despite its university and commuters to the Bay Area population, managed to hold on to its small-town atmosphere. Every July 4th and Christmas, the downtown area was shut down and Turlock turned into "It's a Wonderful Life." For a short time, we could all be George Bailey and savor the friendships and joys of community celebration. Turlock is also a gateway city to Yosemite National Park. Travelers intent on visiting Yosemite might overnight in Turlock, which brings me to this week's topic.

It didn't take me long to realize that for all that I left behind; I gained something of great value in return - the Mississippi River. Mark Twain called it "the lawless river" and its ever-changing passages and vistas have created the backdrop for our lives from one season to the next. I've come to fall in love with the river and whenever we are near the end of Ward Ave., the Pirate, without my asking, drives down to the riverfront. So far, I've discovered driftwood, rusted chains, and barges moored right next to the bank so close you could literally walk up to it. Yesterday I discovered a raft of Blue Bill ducks floating near the riverbank near Bunge. Grain must have scattered into the water creating a feast for the waterfowl. They lifted, glided, and then skittered to a touchdown on the water, moving from one morsel to the next. You really can't plan such an event. Pure luck was my companion in that moment. What an amazing sight.

In my seven months here, I've discovered the river's highs and lows, its moods, and how quickly they can change. I've seen beaches exposed and then covered again. I've learned about levees, locks, dykes, and flood walls, and the differences between them. Barges have become my new trains. We used to live between two train corridors both of which mostly carried freight, everything from petroleum products to cattle. To the east, a commuter train ran between Bakersfield and Sacramento, as well, right down through the middle of the valley. In what might have been my most exciting moment, the replicas of the Nina and the Pinta, two of Christopher Columbus's ships, sailed passed our riverfront. Sadly, that was one of my regrettable misses.

Reading Mark Twain's book, *Life on the Mississippi*, is like reading a history of this mighty river. Riverboats, steamboats, and rafting, live large on the pages of Twain's books. Mule pulled boats were a common mode of transportation. My favorite picture, at the Roundhouse, presents one of these boats which really looked like an oversized raft. Riding on a barge might be a big no-no these days, but mule pulled boat rides can still be had in LaSalle, Illinois and I smell a road trip this year.

Push Tug

Anne Jeffries

What I see from the end of Ward Avenue or from the Caruthersville Bridge, can't begin to unlock the mysteries of our river. But these glimpses *do* unlock my imagination. I've learned to admire, respect, and have a healthy fear of our river. It could become *our* gateway to an improved economy. I can't take enough pictures to satisfy my love for it and I'm betting visitors, if only they had a place to come, would love it too.

Just as Turlock is just two hours from Yosemite, our river is right on our doorstep. The end of Ward Avenue has the beginning of everything. There is a park. Barbecue celebrations happen there. The fishing ramp lures avid fishermen to our little town. This unpolished jewel is our gateway to making an enormous difference in my adopted community. If only others would see it. But from where I sit, newbie that I am, the downtown potential is ignored and left to languish by those who could make a difference. It isn't for want of imagination or will but from empty buildings neglected by owners. Ask yourself, how much more could Caruthersville be if neglect could be overcome and will and imagination were given free rein?

January 29, 2018 - The Music of My Life

Saturday night I enjoyed another evening of music at Little Pizza Heaven listening to The Jax. One-part nostalgia and one-part goofy humor, the Jax is a two-man Jack-in-the-Box of fun embodied by Mike Barnett and Kevin Winstead. It was one of those nights when so many of the songs spoke to me of specific moments in my youth. The rock music of the 60s and 70s is my era, folk, not so much. And country? Never. Back home I had my pick of radio stations for this time period and the so-called Vietnam Era music wailed. Tracks from The Beatles, Rolling Stones, The Mamas and the Papas, and Crosby, Stills, Nash and Young were my playlist. Add to it the Jimi Hendrix Experience, Eric Burden and the Animals, Big Brother and the Holding Company with Janice Joplin, Pink Floyd, and the Moody Blues and my playlist is complete.

Fast forward to the 20-teens, sitting in on Turlock's downtown music scene was not really satisfying. Surrounded by millennials and hipsters just made me feel old and out of place which was too bad. It's not that we outgrew our desire for intimate contact with music; it's that the music outgrew us.

My playlist reflected an era and a regional appeal that didn't include rockabilly with the likes of Elvis, Narvel Felts, or Jerry Lee Lewis. But unexpectedly, KCRV-am radio crept in and lodged into a corner of my heart. Suddenly, old school county music, gospel, and sometimes the blues had my attention. I love listening to the news and the local calendar. I even learned a little something about frog hunting and squirrel hunting. So, when I discovered the local casino was bringing in Narvel Felts, I was game to go. I would hear first-hand why people loved old school rockabilly and country. It wasn't until that night that I learned he was a bit of a local legend, too. The Bootheel claimed him as a favored son. Sweet!

So, now I've been to Little Pizza Heaven and enjoyed The Jax 3 times. I even have a uniform of sorts, a t-shirt I always wear, the Jax original, a T-Rex that can't clap its hands. Their music is right out of my playlist along with some pretty humorous stuff too. And judging by the age range of the pizza loving audience, no one feels too young and out of place. After all, classic rock and blues never go out of style

February 4, 2018 - Shake, Rattle, and Roll

Growing up in California, I lived in the ever-present shadow of the "Big One". We would have the Big One within 30 years. Since "they who know about such things" were measuring from the 1906 San Francisco Earthquake, it seemed to me that by the mid-20th century, we were long overdue. By the time we moved here, I was well into my third 'within 30 years' warning cycle.

Earthquakes are a fact of life in California. The constant, background storm of little 2.0's aren't even noticeable. There is always a whole lot of shakin' going on, even when we don't feel it. Living on the edge of two tectonic plates and more than a few fault lines, well, that is just the way it rolls in California.

But, occasionally, the Golden State likes to make itself felt. The last time we got a good, sound shaking was in 1989 with the Loma Prieta Quake. That one was terrible. Freeway overpasses flattened the cars on the lower level. The San Francisco Embarcadero was no more. That one, all the way out in the Central Valley, I felt. Lines swayed. Plate glass windows rippled. The ground bobbed like a kiddie rollercoaster and for one who doesn't like any kind of rollercoaster, I was terrified and didn't think it would ever stop. The door on my wall clock broke free and opened. The clock door opening was amusing. It was such a small thing but so telling.

There were some sobering and daunting "horrible beauty" photographs to come out of that event. Like all photos that keep records of what happens in the aftermath, there were images that were quintessentially California. They practically scream California at you. Kids skateboarding on makeshift ramps created from uplifted sidewalks might be one such image. So, you can imagine how unimpressed I was by the little 2-point somethings that rattle folks along the New Madrid Fault Line.

It wasn't until I visited the New Madrid Museum that I learned about the Earthquakes of 1811-1812. This quake was a series of quakes and aftershocks that ran from December 1811 through February 1812. The first was in Arkansas estimated to be 7.6. The second, in New Madrid, occurred in January 1812 estimated to be 7.5 and this one swallowed an entire town. The third, in February 1812, created Reelfoot Lake in Tennessee. Anyone who's local knows about Reelfoot and it's one of the first things that visitors or new residents learn about. My respect for the New Madrid Fault was increasing. I was also thinking, "I moved from earthquake central to another quake center? And there are tornados, too? Sheesh!"

But it wasn't until a few weeks ago that I felt and heard one of these fabled quakes. We were hit with a 3.6'er and the lift, clap, and boom I felt and heard was nothing to sneeze at. I also screamed, as if lightning exploding on top of me and accidents with semi's wasn't enough. But hearing it was the scary part for me. Living in the Central Valley of California, our quakes and rumbles were quiet. They roll and come at you in waves. This one felt like two immovable objects moving and then slamming together. I'm sure California quakes aren't quiet for the folks in the thick of them, but for us, it was quiet. Hearing this little 3.6 tremor left me shaking for a while.

So, after seven months here, I've reconciled myself to the not so new normal of my life. I was born in quake country. I will no doubt die in another quake country. I've developed a newfound respect for this little old fault line of yours. It may not be the San Andreas Fault, but it sure packs a punch.

February 10, 2018 - Looking for Sunlight

Days are long and gloomy in the Bootheel during the winter. There are a few things I could be doing but it won't change the fact that in winter, the days are the shortest and feel the longest.

Hours and hours of being alone gets old fast. I tried crocheting today but I did something wrong in the second row, so I tore it all out. Then I planned dinner and read awhile. Thank God for books, but, I'm still restless.

Nikki, my hairdresser, was sick today and called to cancel my appointment. I had been waiting for that appointment for 10 days. Disappointing but oh well. So, I grabbed my jacket and headed out the door.

A good cup of coffee felt just right, and I headed to the Roundhouse. They were closed for the afternoon. Knox, Twister's, and Granddad's Deli had all closed in the past three months, so the next stop was El Carreton. Closed. Last option - Daylight Donuts. Closed. A hot cuppa was not in my immediate future. So, I went to Hays.

Have I ever mentioned that I hate their parking lot? No one knows how to park in this town. I have never felt as unsafe as I do when I'm in the Hays parking lot. Once inside, the contents of my basket started to reflect my state of mind. Apples, oranges, and a pre-made Caesar Salad are the upside. Then I spotted Heavenly Hash ice cream. In the basket, it went. And the coffee was still on my mind, so I bought a small carton of half and half. Neither are good choices and again, oh well.

These luscious pleasures did brighten my mood, if not improve my waistline. And finally, I'm in the check-out line. A Snickers bar jumped into my cart all by its little old self. I can still taste its chocolate chewing flavor. Now, to get that much-desired cup of coffee.

February 12, 2018 - It's Been A Year

Recently, I've been thinking about the passage of time, dates I remember, significant numbers that point us to momentous change. My earliest one goes back 46 years and the damage from that time lingered for many years. Soon after, I left San Diego. Big changes were coming though I could not know it then.

I finished university. Then I met the Pirate and we married in haste. We both knew a good thing when we saw it. I became a mother twice. We bought our first home. I got my last job, one that lasted for 23 years right up to retirement. Nearer in time dates are becoming grandparents three times over and the near death of our daughter and her child.

Along the way, in between all that, Kennedy was assassinated. No one my age is likely to have forgotten where they were when that happened. Then 9/11 occurred. I was so grateful that my father, a Pearl Harbor Survivor, had not live to see that. He died 8 months before that savage moment stained our memories forever.

It wasn't until I started writing this that I realized how many significant events have occurred in my life. My ordinary life seems not so ordinary after all. We all have dates and times we look back on. We only need to reflect, write down just one and the rest will come to the surface naturally. At least, that is how it worked for me. They haven't all been good dates but each, in its own way, held great significance.

One date that had the greatest impact was December 17, 1977. That was the day I decided to take a day trip to the little Southern California mountain community of Idyllwild with a friend. That was the day I met the Pirate. He has shared a lot of my significant dates over the past almost 41 years, but it is the most recent one, now 1 year and 12 days ago that reverberates like a deep bass wind chime.

That Sunday, January 28, 2017, was the night Krista told us that our

#3 grand was on the way and that she and her little family were moving to Tennessee. The door opened wide, welcoming the Pirate back to the place he longed to be. And like Ruth in the Bible, I followed into an unfamiliar world.

Now, nine months have passed by since I started this adventure. The first impacts of change have lessened, and more mundane experience demand my attention, like learning to walk again and not feeling like Quasimodo, ever off balance and slowed down to 33 1/3. Older readers will understand the speed image, younger readers, unless they are fans of vinyl, not likely. And I'm more and more integrating my new reality into daily life and feeling the sharp pangs of saying good-bye to my past. Lent is here; a time of reflection. It's a time to not necessarily give something up as a disciplined offering to God, but more a changing of self, old habits, a cleansing time. Like losing weight and buying new clothes, things fit differently in life now and it's important to discover how to get just the right fit.

February 14, 2018 - Books, Beautiful Books

When I left here four years ago after spending three months on a domestic mission with Sr. Darlene, one of the places that I discovered to be a jewel in the Caruthersville crown was the public library. I discovered it to have a wealth of literary and cultural activities waiting to be shared with the community. I loved going to the library here. Now that we are returned for good, I find that the library has become the heart of this town for me. In the short nine month I've been here, I have been to the library more times than in the nineteen years we lived in Turlock, CA. Yes, they had a nice library, but it had uneven hours and the lure of its presence never clicked with me.

Not so, the Caruthersville Library. From plays to special grant information classes, the Christmas village and Sundays at the movies, renting fishing gear, and genealogical research, this small library has a big heartbeat.

Perusing the stacks, I discovered unread authors and I dove into, heretofore, unknown places. The library also got me to thinking of the place of books in my life. As I reflected on this question, I realized that as a family we had come full circle as a family of book lovers, something that I never thought would happen.

All my adult life, I have never been without a book in my purse. The times it has happened, it has felt as crippling and unnatural as taking my lipstick from my handbag and forgetting to put it back. The Pirate is a reader. He has filled his library with countless books on Civil War history and political and societal issues. Our son, Quanah, has always been a book hound, as my dad would say. To this day I'm amazed that he read, voluntarily, *The Inferno* by Dante Alighieri when he was in high school. It wasn't required reading, it just sounded interesting. Now, in his late '30s, he's still reading the hard stuff, heavy on philosophy, Church history, medieval history, and theology.

It was my daughter I truly despaired of when it came to fostering a love of books. It seemed that no amount of reading to her as a child or encouraging her as a teen would get her to love reading as a recreation. But later, with time, she did start picking up books. She discovered Nicholas Sparks and for her 21st birthday, I gave her all the books he had written up to that point. She read them all. She dove into an autobiography of Anthony Kiedis of the Red-Hot Chili Peppers. Suddenly I had a reading daughter.

Both our children married readers. Quanah's Erin reads the heavy stuff too, but they also read aloud to each other. I remember one memorable night I called them, and they were reading one of the Harry Potter books to each other or maybe it was "Lord of the Rings". Anyway, the habit continues to this day and I find it very old-fashioned and very, very, endearing. Krista's husband, Adrian, reads self-improvement books, inspirational success stories, and modern Catholic writers for living a righteous life and being a good man, a good husband, and a good father.

The thing that makes me the happiest though is our grandson, Sebastian. Seb, at 3 1/2, *loves* books. He "reads" them daily. His little brother, Matteo seems to have picked up on reading as well but at 2, he's still too busy being a toddler. And Karolina, at 4 months, will no doubt click with reading. She is already showing signs of wanting to keep up with her brothers.

And now, birthdays and Christmases all seem to center around books and journals. Book giving has become the number one choice for thoughtful gifting, and it extends to our friends and other family loved ones, too. Visiting libraries and bookstores constitutes a good date night for Don and me. It's a satisfying feeling, at this late stage in life, that our children will never have to be stumped on what to get mom and dad for Christmas. Books are the glue of our lives. When things fall apart or we need to just escape, there is always a book to retreat to.

This week I have two books to mail off to Krista and Adrian. One is *The Case for Jesus*. The other, for Adrian, is entitled *Resucito Jesus*

Realmente de Entre los Muertos? At a time in their lives when disposable income is at a premium, I'm quietly happy that I can provide them with books as they continue to stir the pot and make the glue of their own lives.

Dedicated to The Pirate who

keeps me supplied in journals.

February 19, 2018 - A Season for Reflection

I've been pondering Lent this week; most especially of the care for others and recognizing God's presence within everyone. Matthew 25: 31-46 tells us we will be judged on what we do and don't do for others. Jesus is very specific about it, too. Lately, I find myself more conscious of this than ever. Perhaps it has something to do with aging but frankly, I attribute my current deeply reflective turn of mind to my church community here; a church community that fosters prayer, adoration, education, and community in action for its members. For the first time, after a lifetime of multiple moves and being a member of many parishes, I'm experiencing Bible study and a love of my faith in a way that is deeply meaningful and personal.

So, how do we respond to Matthew's Gospel of the Lord? How far do we take His instructions? How do we recognize the difference between enabling and truly helping? Should we try to recognize this or is it only for us to provide the perceived need? Do you give the drug-addicted drugs? Do you give food to the obese never thinking about its value for their bodies? Do you pay a person not to work or ignore the over-indulgences of alcohol addiction and sex addiction? And, what about social alienation? How do you help to find balance and stop self-abuse?

The answer is easy. Listen to Christ's words. Sadly, the world around us makes it complicated. So, how do you reject worldly complications and help? Do you choose one way? Or, do you choose many ways? Where do you help? How do you help?

Each of us has a station in life but we don't have to stay there. It's only a starting place wherein we are open to accepting help, open to being aware of seeing the needs of others and act; understanding that movement from our starting place can be upward or downward. We can rise or sink into the abyss squandering the possibilities of life. Movement is as much physical as it is spiritual. We can remain at a physical low while acting in a way that elevates us spiritually just as a person more, well-placed can squander his gifts and be lost in a sea of selfishness and disdain or even fear.

We are given only one life to get it right but in that single lifetime, we have many opportunities. We can start out wrong but have countless chances to grow in the love of God by giving service to others. We can also start out well-placed but, in the end, fall into selfishness or despair and loss of hope.

For me, there are two simple keys. One is to recognize God's presence in my life and the lives of others. The other key is to act. And, it's not up to me to judge the value of my actions. That I will leave for God.

March 5, 2018 - The Shape of Wind

So far, since arriving here, I have heard an earthquake, I've watched a river rise, and I have even seen a funnel cloud being pulled along to somewhere by the cloud that birthed it. But in all my life, I can honestly say that I've never seen the shape of wind.

Back home in sunny California, the Golden State lived up to its name. The weather was generally pleasing with the rain interspersed evenly across the seasons, droughts notwithstanding. Being in the Central Valley, we did have our share of wind and I loved it. Allergies didn't plague me so a walk on a windy day was pure heaven. On the edge of the valley, against the foothills, the wind would blow through the Pacheco Pass or push up over the western hills from the Coastal Mountains and pour down into the valley. There was nothing to stop its forward motion.

Usually, by the time it reached Turlock, it had spread out across the farmland and had become a soft breeze. But whether strong or gentle, it was usually always around. Spring was especially beautiful. The wind would blow through the almond orchards and for a few weeks we would have a faintly pink tinted petal fall as almond blossoms fluttered to the ground.

For the most part, winds didn't do much damage in my area. We did have our random tree falls but generally, they were not a usual occurrence. It wasn't until I arrived here that I even knew there was such a thing as a straight-line wind, a wind that blew horizontally to the ground. A quick Google search educated me on the wisdom of respecting a thunderstorm wind. The whole idea of wind and its sister, rain, took on an entirely new meaning for me.

The first thing I learned to do was walk the front and back yards after a good "gully washer", as my dad used to like to say. All manner of stuff was found - tree limbs, twigs, pummeled baby birds (that was a hard one), bird nests, unhatched eggshells, and small critters have all ended up in our yard.

But, next to all this, it was my vision of the shape of the wind that totally knocked me out. Remember February 24th, just twelve days ago? The Pirate and I were at Little Pizza Heaven enjoying our monthly music night with The Jax. We went out knowing the rain would be rough and a tornado watch had been announced. Sometime into the evening, it turned into a tornado warning though there was some disagreement about that because the sirens never went off.

We lost the streetlights momentarily and when they returned, I got my first look at the shape of wind when it's blasting through a horizontal rainfall. The swirls and sweeps and rushes of the wind are visible, exciting, and dramatic. It's like watching a flamenco dancer burning the ground with icy heat. Of course, I was mainly clueless as to what this could all mean but I certainly learned the next day when I read of two tornadoes directly north and directly south of us, both about equal distances from us. To say we were right in the middle of it, would not put too fine a point on it.

So now I have two elements of nature to respect: respect the river and respect the wind. Oh, and did I mention that we lost electrical power for about four or five hours? Oh, yes, we did. And now we are talking about getting a generator.

March 6, 2018 - The River Has Peaked

Well, I finally made it down to the river today. The Pirate went with me because my climbing days are over thanks to a pair of very bad knees. He climbed up onto the flood wall, nimble salt that he is. The word on the street says the river is peaking today at 41.5 feet. It should be back down to pre-flood stage by March 20.

The end of Ward Avenue has a nice little park and loading ramp for fishing boats. The Bunge Grain Elevator is right next to it. The picture here shows the park and pavilion all overwhelmed by Old Muddy. Farther down and away from the park, the land is lower, and the water is almost all the way to the base of the flood wall.

Flood collage

Anne Jeffries

March 12, 2018 - Slowing Down

Like all things, slowing down has shades of meaning. Humidity may slow me to a standstill at lower temperatures here and the mosquitoes are a new problem I had my first battles with last summer. But other areas of life have pushed hard at my busyness index. Shopping is a big area that has changed. Shopping takes planning. Shopping takes deciding. Shopping asks me if I need to take a short jaunt or a longer, day-long event. I've opted mostly for the short jaunt mainly because I am reluctant to stray too far off. This desire to not drive much beyond Hayti, on my own, is a mystery that came with our arrival. After 9 months, I've decided not to fight it. But not straying far has allowed me some benefits.

Spending less on impulse purchases is an obvious big benefit but I have also come to like the space of time that now happen between Starbucks runs. In nine months, I've been to Starbucks twice. Considering that a Starbucks run was an almost daily occurrence in my former life, this is a slowdown that could be measured in latte light years if there was such a thing.

Slowing down with people is another big one. People are mostly friendly here. I chalk that up to Southern politeness which I like very much. But for a person who comes from a world where someone can become an "instant" friend, navigating the waters of Southern politeness can be tricky. Family members, long gone, are still present in current conversation as if they were just in the next room and would appear at any moment. Memory is kept alive here. My family is small and scattered all over. We're in California, West Virginia, Wisconsin, New York, Colorado, Indiana, Tennessee, and Oregon. Many on that extended list live in Wisconsin and New York and most of them I haven't seen since childhood. The rest are my immediate family or in-law connections.

California has one, West Virginia has one. Tennessee and Indiana have five and two respectively. Any way you cut it; my family is small.

The Pirate was an only child. He calls this place home but he's probably just one of a handful of people who have few family roots here. And, those who might remember his parents are themselves very old. That string of memory is being stretched very thin.

Of course, there is that pesky old thing called aging. It is inescapable and I may look in the mirror and see a woman holding together fairly well but the evidence of slowing down is constantly present. My knee tells me all the time that I am no spring chicken (yes, I used that cliché)

So, I slow down and figure out the Plan B of how to get on in daily life. Do I want pictures of the other side of the flood wall? Pirate is on duty. In fact, he's on duty for a lot these days, God love him. And, I'm slowing down to savor the change, to observe a new world, to encounter people in a new way. Slowing down allows for clarity and depth of meaning and understanding. Slowing down is very much like reading the Bible. The slower and more carefully you read it, the more meaning you find, the more connections you make, and the more applicable its lessons become.

March 19, 2018 – Just Do It

My local newspaper readers might feel they are hearing an echo from the Jeffries household this week, but the importance of voting is a bit of a passion for both the Pirate and me. Back in California, we generally felt very hopeless about the outcome of a race or proposition. Because of the extreme and well-moneyed liberal stance of California, its high population, and the maldistribution of representatives at a state level, we pretty much knew which way any voting wind would blow. In a single generation, we saw many social issues become positively draconian in their impact on rural California and on traditional values.

I'd lived long enough to see respect for individual rights and hope for positive change for all swing in a direction that might find a balance, for a moment, at least. Then the loud, insistent yell of special interests eroded that moment and in a matter of just a few voting cycles, pretty much anything goes now in that late great state.

Here, Caruthersville can be viewed as a microcosm of California. We have losses to our economy, high unemployment, high poverty rates, blacks, whites, and Hispanics, churches galore, and public social services. I have noticed that people do build bridges between the various groups and churches to effectively serve the community where local government cannot, but we need more than that. We need job skills and training. We need industry and retail merchants. We need to imagine a more beautiful Caruthersville, take advantage of our ideally suited location for arts, music, and a boardwalk of shops that draw in out of town visitors.

I know I've been here less than a year and many of you might tsk-tsk me, conceding to past disappointments. But the things I list above are what gives hope to a community, and even better, unify a community. Personally, I think the economic downward spiral is as bad, if not worse, than the tornado of 2006. Yes, that tornado caused instant and devastating damage to families, some of who I know now, and business and the greater community, but, the long, sustained, quiet, insidious downward pull of the local economy is a killer of community. Willing and creative minds need to go out in the world and push for what we need, what our entire community needs.

So, ask yourself, how do you view the past recent years? How have you been affected personally; what about your neighbors? How often have you felt the sting of neglect because maybe you didn't live in the "right" neighborhood? Based on what I've seen and heard since moving here, I think even some of our own city leaders can testify to that question and what that sting may feel like.

When I lived in California, I was accused of having an island mentality. It took a lot to get me out of Turlock. I had everything I needed there and more. Coming here, I learned right away I had to throw off that kind of thinking but, you know, it's just not that easy and I'm very nearly paralyzed when it comes to driving beyond Hayti. I think when Wal-Mart closed many of you, especially the elderly and impoverished, felt stranded, too. Well, you *were,* and more than a year has passed since its closing and nothing has happened, absolutely zero. In fact, Absolute Zero's definition should be extended to include a before and after of Caruthersville, with the closing of Wal-Mart.

So, come April 3rd, *vote.* Vote for yourself, vote for your neighbors. Vote for your community. Take the long view. We can build something and all we need is effective leadership from the top down. We need unity, communication, and most of all, we need *will.* If you think there is even the remotest possibility of not voting on April 3rd, vote absentee. Go to the courthouse. The last day you can vote absentee is Monday, April 2nd. Don't think your preferred candidate will win without your vote. That is how candidates lose elections. The voting population here is small. Your vote can't get lost in a sea of numbers here.

So, to borrow a Nike ad line:
"Just Do It!"

April 2, 2018 - Musings on Fearfulness

Have you ever met a person of whom you became so aware of their hidden anger that you were made fearful and ran? Of course, you have. They are out there, lots of them, and when they reveal their true colors, fight or flight takes over. I was a flight kind of girl for most of my life.

But while musing this morning on someone I used to know through blogging, I realized I wasn't fearful anymore. There isn't anything she could do to me except continue using her words if I continued to let her in. So, in 2008, "flight" me slammed that particular door.

Fast-forward to 2018 and here I am asking myself why, ten years later, I'm even thinking about her. Well, the answer is simple and complicated at the same time. First, I'm 10 years older, and second, I am closer to God, literally and figuratively, and I have found a source of strength I didn't have when I was younger. Getting through the second part was complicated. Growing in wisdom and strength is hard work and some of us take the hard roads to get through the complicated times of our lives. Do you recognize yourself here? I sure do.

But since moving here, something wonderful has happened. All the lessons about not being afraid of people or just life, in general, have been pushed aside. Granted, I've been working on this for a lot longer than the 10 months we've lived here but certain things started to disappear in my life, things like conflict, doubt, wariness, disappointment, hopelessness, isolation, too many choices, feeling the world is too big or the choices too many, and a foolish desire to be young again, are just a few things.

These feelings have been replaced by a community of both town and church, peace, hope, possibility, a scaled down world of fewer choices, welcome, and gratitude that I have been blessed with a long life.

Two things I tangibly gained by moving here are the river and my own back porch. Living in the Central Valley of California, the ocean was an occasional treat. Here, driving to the river is a daily blessing. A long time ago when my dad was overseas or away during the Korean Conflict, we lived in Northern Wisconsin with my grandparents. They had a great front porch. I loved hanging out there. Now I have my own back porch and I love sitting out there enjoying my birds, my squirrels, and the sound of the wind in the trees.

These two things plus my church community took me down the last long strip of road that got me away from fear and into a closer relationship with God. And, with this experience, I have the strength to continue chasing fearfulness away, because as we all know, the things that haunt us are never too far from us, are they?

April 7, 2018 - Easter Renewed and Renewed and Renewed, Again

Since moving to Missouri from California last summer, I've been given countless ways of taking a second look at my former world and what my life has become since then.

Lent and Easter are one of the frames of my life and the celebration of Easter always looms largely. From the childhood excitement of the annual spring ensemble to the rearing of my own children and instilling in them the importance of Easter, and right up to today, it's celebration and importance has come full bloom in my life. Easter isn't just another feast day. It's the culmination of what we believe and like Christ in the human period of His life, we His children, each arrive at an understanding of His sacrifice in our own time.

In our last years in California we had settled in a parish in a small farming community. This church community was about 80% Latino with more than a few members living in the shadows and so it was hard to build bridges across the cultural divide. People were comfortable with the way things were.

When Don and I, two non-Spanish speakers, worked two summers at a migrant camp teaching English as a second language all that started to change for us. As our faces became more familiar, within the Latino community, we were regarded less with distant wariness. It was an object lesson on the importance of bridge building, shared language not required. We were also shown how we fit into the larger parish community. We were gifted with a glimpse of the possibility of what can be found in unity.

I see that possibility now forming and maturing in ways unexpected and welcoming. As members of Sacred Heart parish in Caruthersville, Missouri, the experience of community has been enhanced from the microscopic to the more powerful community element that we are. Easter here is simple, elegant, multi-cultural, multi-economic, multi-age, and in some cases even multi-faith. The smallness of our community, expanded by visitors from out of town and twice a year Catholics, embraced an intimacy and expectancy that is heightened by this somewhat larger gathering.

Each day, the Triduum grew in attendance and there were no strangers in the church. Unlike larger parishes, no one left unnoticed. Small bridges were appearing everywhere. I've often been left wondering how to extend this feeling. Here in the very small parish of Sacred Heart, Caruthersville, a way has been found. One very overworked priest overseeing two parishes and one grade school, not to mention a myriad of other responsibilities, combined with a core group of faithful members, participate to continually give the gift of community to one and all.

In California, the phrase, "We are an Easter people" is commonly heard in our church around this time of the year. It's interesting to note that I have not heard this phrase once during this Easter season. Thinking about the depth of community we felt this Easter season in our new home, the phrase seems to fade into meaninglessness. What we are, in fact, is a community. The Resurrection is our highest event, the culmination of our faith. What I felt this year, in a deeply profound way, was the resurrection of the meaning of community. What I really felt like shouting was, "We are a family. We are a community." We can carry this feeling throughout the year. And most importantly, we are capable of breathing life into the idea of community and making it grow and flourish in the larger community of our small town. It lingers quietly here, simply waiting for us.

April 16, 2018 - Touching What is Old

History and geography were my favorite subjects in high school. They found their perfect blend in the study of anthropology when I was in college. These two blended subjects always led me to what was old, interesting, and filled with memories.

When I was in my mid to late '20s, it wasn't unusual to find myself on a long weekend away from home traveling to the desert, a developing urban area, or the Baja California coast of Mexico for plant collecting and archaeological discoveries. The Southern California coastal Indian and inland Indian cultures had a healthy trade route between themselves and along the coast. Political barriers didn't exist then and people freely moved from one place to another, evidence of their passages found in the shared trade goods of the time.

While I studied mainly California Indian culture, I also had a passing study experience with the Mound Builders of the Mid-West and the South. The young woman I was then never imagined that 40 plus years later she would find herself married to a southern Missouri man and eventually would become friends with a woman who had a mound on land right next to her home and farm. Something old from my youth was imposing itself on my older years and I was fascinated. My mind is still alive to the lure of history and geography and I took up a brief study of the Mound Builder culture in this area. There is really nothing like a sense of history to solidify one's relationship to a place. No, I'm not from here but my story will become a little piece of what makes up the story of the Bootheel.

So, here I am today and touching "old" is affecting me in unforeseen ways. I talked about church community last week and the opportunities offered by my new community have led me to an interesting solution regarding my mindset of the place of clutter in my life.

The upside of my clutter is that when we moved, most of it got packed away, thereby making the Pirate very happy. Yes, some of it was tossed but on reflection, not nearly as much as needed to be. But, hey! I wasn't there yet. The downside is that it's still mostly all packed away nearly a year after arriving here. I really can't ignore it anymore. So, the solution is what?

My attraction to Benedictine spiritually has been a presence in my life for several years and I'm now reading a book written over a period that spanned the 5th and 6th century) entitled, "The Rule of Saint Benedict". The reality of clutter packed or otherwise, in my life has now reached the "I will not be ignored" stage. Between the early reading of the book and the imposition of the" old" from my younger years imposing itself on my new "old stuff" reality, I discovered quickly how simple decluttering could become.

Simplicity and orderliness lead to a calmness and opens pathways to God that might otherwise be blocked. I ask myself now how something makes me feel. Or, perhaps I ask myself how long it has been since I used the thing. When was the last time I even saw it? Do I remember where I found it? Will I use it again? Is it one of those things always in the back of my mind interfering with my prayer life or, equally bad, interfering with my ability to enjoy my leisure? Ignoring a problem doesn't make a problem go away. It simply simmers until it gets bumped and then it boils over.

All my stuff is so old. I've had it for so long. Some of it is family treasures that have gone from one life to another and now me. These things will never go and eventually will be disbursed but, for the most part, I can get rid of at least half of the rest of it and never notice its absence afterward.

Therefore, following a few ideas gleaned from my reading, I am now tackling the really old stuff in my physical day to day life. I find myself starting to feel ready to let go and all it took was a crazy journey of oddly disparate pieces of my life and their unexpected connectedness to get here. Yesterday I let go of a tablecloth. Painless, it was, when I accepted that it had no purpose and held no family history. If the rest of this process goes as painlessly, I will count the sweeping out of the

Anne Jeffries

unnecessary "old" as a success. The Pirate will thank me. My children will thank me, later. As you know, we all have a later. And, I will thank me because I have the satisfaction of knowing that I am doing something that is pleasing to the Lord as I let go of the material things weighing me down, thereby making more room for Him and for my little community I call my family.

April 30, 2018 - Why I Like the River So Much

All my adult life, my dream was to live near the Pacific Ocean. Growing up in San Diego does that to a person. But choices in life led me one place and then the next and the watery dream shrank to the occasional well-planned visit. But I've been very lucky in that my life has been bookended by water. The ebb-time of my life has placed me next to water again in a most unexpected way.

THE RIVER

Watery highway
Heavy with commerce
Endlessly flowing through our lives
Flowing through our own busy days

You are a place of peace
A place to meet
A place to dream
A place to pray

Rejuvenation and healing
A place of quiet refuge from noise
Seasonal beauty, its colors
Show us rivers within the River

Awe-inspiring power sweeps
The old and uprooted, passing us by
Treasures left on your shores
Find homes, being renewed as we
We are renewed

Teased by your abundant
Strength, I step back and let
You flow through me.

Sunday marked an afternoon of prayer at the River. We joined with people of the United Kingdom and Ireland who gathered on their coastlines and we all prayed for peace for our community, our nation, and our world.

May 8, 2018 - I Joined A Book Club

I joined the book club, at the Caruthersville Library, last month and as a fully-fledged bookworm, this should have been something that wasn't new to me. But, like so much of my Bootheel experience during this first year, I had never joined a book club before now and I had to wonder why.

I love books. I talk books with friends over coffee. I collect books and have several editions of my two favorites - *Jane Eyre* and *The Secret Garden*. I learn from books. I travel with books. My world is opened wide by books. So why have there been no book clubs in my past?

Have you ever met an extrovert who is always on the watch inside? Well, that would be me. I like people but I've also been easily disappointed by them. Of course, that was way back, when having expectations of people just naturally led most often to disappointment and it is our experiences that form us. But just because we are let down doesn't mean we have to continue being let down. Entering any activity with few expectations leads to better outcomes, at least for me. Suddenly, people seemed more reliable.

Whatever the reason for the disappointment, the lesson was to go my own way and I pretty much chose to do that all my adult life. My circle of friends was small and loyal, and I was happy with that. Then I move here.

I know you've heard it before but living here is very different for me. The Pirate fit right in. He knew the ground rules. After a year of living here, I've learned that my California sensibilities don't necessarily fit. So, over the course of this year, I've met a lot of people, fit myself into my own special writing and visiting place, rubbed shoulders, quite literally sometimes, at city council meetings, enjoyed library events, and getting to know my church community. And most importantly, I had the river and the never-ending barge life to comfort and soothe me through my homesick times. I finally felt ready to test the waters, so to speak, and take the pulse of joining a club and what I found was so satisfying.

The group is small. There are no right or wrong answers, no opinions or "takes" on a point of plot or character that outshine what other members have to say. Perhaps all book clubs are like this but by the time I retired from work, joining a social group was completely not my thing. People disappointed. The lesson of a year of living in Caruthersville changed all that. The lesson was having no expectations.

When I arrived at my first meeting, I had not read the book since the decision to go was last minute. No problem. I met some interesting people. The discussion was lively and after my second visit, I felt my own creative powers being pushed. There are more than a few writers here and I started thinking that having a writers' workshop one day at the library might be a way to push to the next level in my own writing. Even though I've written on and off my whole life, I've never shared it beyond writing on my blogs. Then I moved here.

I recently gave my daughter some advice as she started out on a new endeavor of her own. I told her to take small steps. Don't jump in deep and expect to swim. Find your success in a small way. Find your comfort zone. It's funny how words for the young can be equally valuable for the not so young.

Sharing my writing here has been a door I was willing to walk through to take my own steps a bit farther away from my own comfort zone. And, believe me, it was scary. Joining a book club, sharing my thoughts and opinions about another writer's writing has been a similar experience. I haven't had too much to say yet, but I have found that I may be able to comfortably do the social group thing after all since the welcome I've received, like jumping into a heated pool, has been warm and reassuring.

May 14, 2018 - Graduations, Big and Small, and that Talk with God

Fifteen years have passed since I attended what I imagined would be my last high school graduation. It was in 2003 that my youngest took her walk across the stage and into her future. God had answered my prayers and I sat back and relaxed, for about a minute.

Before long, I was having another one of my talks with God. I acknowledged that He had answered all my prayers and I was beyond grateful but suddenly I saw a long path into the future and there was still a whole lot of mothering work I needed to do. There was college, smoothing the bumps of young adulthood, marriages, and grandchildren looming into the future. And just like that, I had a lot more praying to do and wisdom and reassurances to dispense.

And sure enough, the smoothing happened, the marriages arrived, and grands appeared. There was a lot to live for. Of course, these events weren't simply a matter of ticking off a box. Each was a gift and I was grateful to have these joys. Life was perfect. I had been given everything I had prayed for. Then I found myself, most unexpectedly, at another high school graduation.

The instant lesson I learned is that high school graduation in a small town is a pretty big deal. Amongst this graduating class of 88 students, everyone knew someone even if you weren't related. How could you not? Even we knew a few of the students and we have only been here for a year.

A few things stood out for me that made this small-town graduation uniquely different, though. For one thing, the entire town seemed to be involved. There were fireworks at the end thanks to the Caruthersville Fire Department; the local police kept things orderly, there were graduation baccalaureates at many of the churches which was something I had never heard of, graduating seniors walked the grade school hallways, and there was the tossing of the mortarboards. When my kids graduated, there were nearly 900 students in each class, cap tossing wasn't allowed, though my now 38-year-old son confessed to me this Mother's Day weekend that he and his friends did, indeed toss their caps and fireworks were absolutely forbidden. *And, walking an elementary school hallway?* Really, just think about that for a moment. Our old town was large enough that another high school was eventually built, and the dreaded annual traffic nightmare was somewhat abated.

So, experiencing this annual rite of passage here without a child or grandchild of my own to be seen got me to thinking and I had another one of my talks with God. This time I asked that He keep me around long enough and in good enough health that I could enjoy at least three more high school graduations. After all, I had three grands, the youngest of who is just 8 months old. I really, really need at least 18 more years. Considering I'm what is called an "old" grandma, this is no small request. And, while I'm at it, Lord, it would be nice to be a great-grandmother. I'm sure God must be thinking by now that I'm a broken record.

May 21, 2018 - It's Been A Year

This Friday, May 25th, we will have been in Caruthersville for one full year. The change for the Pirate has been amazing. He is like a different man. Oh, the basics are still there, first and foremost, his single-mindedness, but socially, he is a man I never knew in California. And, in all the changes I've experienced in my own first year here, this change, his emergence into a more social person, has been the biggest one for me. More so, of all the social changes that I've noted, the biggest one is that he laughs more. A lot more.

So now I march into my second year here and a lot has happened. First off, let's talk about coffee. Daily Starbucks visits are no more, but the Roundhouse has a decent brew and I can spend an hour or two there reading, writing, and visiting. I also discovered Sweet Tea quite by accident (choke). Sorry folks, but I'm Team Unsweet. The closest my tea ever gets to tasting sweet is when I have an Arnold Palmer and somehow the lemonade/iced tea combo is okay if it's made with iced tea, unsweet.

The library makes me feel very special. The ladies got to know me right away. I'll go in now to pick up a book I've had on hold and I'm likely to find another one waiting for me with it. Like a mysterious Facebook algorithm, they know what interests me and so far, they have been right.

I have a sense of loneliness here but not of being alone. The loneliness comes from the loss of all that I knew and the occasional yearning for a visit back to my old home isn't uncommon. But here I have found easygoing friendliness and welcome that has born the fruit of invitations to clubs, service organizations, and church groups.

Life speeds up here during the summer. Yes, it's *hot* and life speeds up. Grandparents visiting or being visited by grands are a summer staple. And, wow, do the women here travel. My Facebook feed is alive

Anne Jeffries

with travel adventures to please even the most deeply rooted armchair traveler.

The first-time events came at me fast and furious last summer. I experienced thunder so loud, it made me scream, not squeal, but outright scream. I had no idea I could hit such high notes. I was a passenger in a car rear-ended by a semi. I saw my first funnel cloud sailing peacefully across the sky, not the least bit interested in making a fuss for us mere human below.

I *heard* an earthquake. None of that San Andreas rolling swaying for me anymore. The New Madrid fault had decided to introduce itself to me with a clap and a bang.

I toured a cotton gin *and* climbed up into a cotton picker. Can you say *wow*? The picker ride was like an old E-Ticket ride at Disneyland. I fell in love with your river and the barges and push tugs. Flood watching became my daily winter activity. Now if I could just get a ride on a tug.

I cried over lost baby birds, blown from their nests during foul weather. I love my bunnies, birds, and squirrels that live in our yards. And this week I discovered that we have finches, too. Splash and dash rainfalls add to humidity. Sideways rain adds drama to life.

JAX and Jammin' at Joy's, not to mention Radio 1370-am and its old school music and radio shows have brought music to my personal front burner with regular dates noted on my Android calendar.

I tried my hand at canning. Once. My kitchen is too small so, no, I won't be canning again. And what I didn't know about mice before I moved here, I sure know now. And speaking of learning, I'm learning a second language. It's called Southern.

Voting and high school graduation are almighty community events unlike anything back home. Back in California, strangers gathered in line, voted, and departed. It was all very serious back there. Here? Neighbors met. People laughed and chatted. Gossip about what was happening at the other Wards was the main theme.

Graduating seniors, for that one moment, became everyone's children. Their dreams were on the cusp of come true. While we can't predict how long they may have to wait for the dreams to unfold; I do know the Pirate had to wait a lifetime for his to be fulfilled.

So, what are my hopes, dreams, and goals for this second year of my new life? Two things instantly come to mind:

1. I *will* drive out of town, farther than Hayti, this year, and
2. I will finally, finally, get upstairs and finish that room that has been patiently waiting for me.

Summer Returns

June 14, 2018 - Let's Talk About Swimming and Shopping

I discovered a couple of things this week. The first is that I am brave enough to batter down the barriers that make up my comfort zone. One of my major comfort zone challenges is entering a public pool area in a bathing suit. Yeah. Just. Don't. Go. There. That is until I moved to Caruthersville.

Did you know that you have an indoor pool heated to 82 degrees year-round? Well, I'm here to say that this pool experience has been awesome. It took me a year to get there. I am highly resistant to public pools. A certain local retired Judge can attest to that. He told me six months ago to hit the pool and that would fix my knee up fast. Did I listen to him? No. But then, Mayor Sue started badgering me and she brooked no excuses. So, what if I didn't have a bathing suit. Buy one. Check out QVC.

Well, the Judge was right. And, even though I didn't find a suit at QVC, I *did* find one elsewhere. Once that was accomplished, I dove in. Literally. I must admit, my knee is feeling better and would have no doubt recovered by now had I listened sooner to smarter minds than my own. But I got there and I'm not looking back. Despite my "take my time" nature, I was quick to realize the recreation center and its pool would be seeing a lot of me.

So, what about timing? For me, 8:30 - 9:30 a.m.is perfect. I don't want to be in a group so an 8:30 arrival works. Plus, I have a swim buddy that likes that hour as well. It's quiet. There are few people and the ones who are there are all oldsters like me. No kids. Don't get me wrong. I like kids but not when I'm swimming.

My second discovery of the week was so far inside my comfort zone that I'm almost giddy with joy. One of my regular fun things I did back home was head out into the countryside to visit all the part-time hobby arts and crafts shops that occupied space at several of the orchards and dairy farms that surrounded us. These charming, mostly seasonal shops were filled with home goods, antiques, foods, and painting classes, enough to satisfy anyone who thinks boutique shopping is the only way to shop. So, when I saw a Sassy's advertisement on Facebook this past Friday, I *had* to go and see it for myself. First problem, the Pirate was out with the car and I had no idea when he would return. Second problem, the little shop closed at 2 p.m. and it was 1 p.m. when I saw the announcement on my feed. And, since the Pirate doesn't usually take his phone with him, I was stuck. He arrived home at 1:40 and I flew out the door. I knew where Highway U was but that address number looked awfully high. But I went for it and I'm so glad I did.

Pat Thrasher and Mitzi Leek have been friends for thirty years. It seemed more than natural to join in a partnership and create a shop featuring old furniture that has been refurbished, sweet collectables, jewelry, and miscellaneous treasures. Their dream is starting small and out of town for now. The big dream is to have a bricks and mortar shop in town offering up a relaxing haven for boutique shopping. They also offer up yummy cookies and bake goods. Simple, homemade, and tasty delights are always on the menu.

For now, they are open on Thursday and Friday from 10 a.m. to 2 p.m. Park in front and go around to the back. You will probably see the shop namesake, Sassy the Goat, along the way but no worries; she's a sweetie. In fact, I heard that she is a bit of a goat personage around here. In her younger and slimmer days (didn't we all have those, ladies?) she would ride in the truck and go everywhere with her Daddy.

So, visit them. Show Pat and Mitzi some love. If they get enough traffic on Thursday-Friday sales, who knows? We may have a sweet little downtown boutique to add to the scattered treasures that already exist down here.

June 23, 2018 - I'm Back

Taking a couple of weeks off refreshed me. Along the way, I had some interesting experiences and met some nice people.

Caruthersville has a surprisingly deep well of talent. Not only can we claim established artists such as Gary Lucy and Pennie Brantley, we can also claim bragging rights to well-known comedian and actor, Cedric the Entertainer. It doesn't take long, after meeting him, to realize that he is, certifiably, one of the good guys.

Someone else I met recently is a gentleman named Benny Bell. I've always been partial to the dance arts and was glad when my son decided to study dance for a few years. It's good to see Mr. Bell battling his way back from injuries. I hope to see you dancing again, though perhaps not quite so dramatically, and inspiring another generation of male dancers.

Alongside the artists, dancers, and actors, we also have a fair number of published writers. Ann Stokes (born a slave) contributed to the Federal Writers' Project: Slave Narrative Project, Vol. 10 written and compiled from 1936-1938. One of our current City Councilmen, Josh Rittenberry, has written three books and is working on a fourth. His books can be found on Smashwords. Our librarian, Teresa Tidwell, is in print. You can find her on Amazon. And I have a book of meditations through Blurb Books.

We can also call R&B, Soul, and Jazz singer Donna Hightower our own singer/songwriter who recorded on the Decca and Capital labels. Miss Hightower also had a successful career in Europe. She passed away in 2013. Also, in the music scene from Caruthersville is Reggie Young, a leading sessions musician who has recorded with Elvis, Herbie Mann, Dionne Warwick, and Johnny Cash, just to name a few. At 81, Mr. Young is still making music in the Memphis area.

Also, to be noted is the screenwriter, Wendell Mayes. While not born in Caruthersville, he almost was since he was born in Hayti, right next door. That is close enough to claim bragging rights. His first writing credit was the Billy Wilder film, *The Spirit of St. Louis*. Not too shabby for a first film credit. He also wrote, *Anatomy of a Murder* for which he received an Oscar nomination in 1960. His name can be found on many notable and recognizable film titles including *The Poseidon Adventure* (the original one). Mr. Mayes died in 1992.

And, finally, while not an entertainer, I had to include James Oliver, because I just think this is a very big deal. Mr. Oliver (born in 1914) was a zoologist, herpetologist, and educator who served as director of the American Museum of Natural History - NYC, directed the New York Zoological Park (now the Bronx Zoo) and was director of the New York Aquarium. Mr. Oliver passed away in 1981.

While busying myself learning about C'ville's many notable individuals from the past, I also managed to finally get myself back upstairs. Moving is hard work and boring work. Sorting, organizing, and tossing is a seriously boring business. This is especially true because of the neverendingness of it. Yes, I made up that word and told spellcheck to ignore it.

Fortunately, since moving here, shopping has slowed considerably. My love of thrifting is pretty much a thing of the past and this makes the Pirate very happy.

I continue to learn that plans can be changed in an instant when a 100% chance of rain in pronounced, *not* predicted, and then turns into a piffle.

I've also learned that it's a good idea to call ahead to the produce businesses to make sure they are opened. I've gone on produce trips twice now and both times left disappointed. Thank you, rain, for delaying the bounty that is peaches and pears.

The best part of this little break, however, was my growing acquaintance with fireflies. They have been stirring up a lot of desert night skies memories and I believe I'll be writing more about that next week.

June 29, 2018 - The Condition of Light

I've been thinking about light lately. I remember, back home, there was a particular crossroad that had a certain quality of light from time to time that took my breath away. Maybe it was an especially clean air day combined with a recently irrigated field. I really don't know. All I am sure of is that when I saw it, it was special and for many years that crossroad was one of my happy places. I had learned to watch for it. Light makes us feel safe. We know exactly where we are. We don't necessarily have a sense of direction that tells us where to go (yes, I'm raising my hand) but we can see what is around us including the slow movement of the sun as it points the way.

Darkness is a different matter. When a bird recently flew into the pool area at the local recreation center, I couldn't imagine how Nikki, the lifeguard, would show it the way out. But the next work morning, Nikki located the bird. Yes, it was still alive, having survived the weekend enclosed with no access to food. She turned out all the interior lights and opened the side door to the dawning light. That scrap of light was all it took to orient the little guy and out he flew. I bet he was very hungry.

The night is a different matter. I'm not afraid of darkness though I must admit that lightning makes me very uneasy. Thunder and lightning were not a storm staple back home. Oh, we had intermittent rumbles and flashes but nothing like here where the night can turn into an eerie sort of daylight that keeps coming at you in waves until the storm passes.

When I was a child, we drove cross country several times and my earliest memory is associated with desert night skies and blinking stars. There is absolutely nothing so breathtaking for me as a desert sky on a moonless night. The stars inhabit the sky like fireflies that never go out. We didn't have fireflies where we moved from and I find this curious.

The Central Valley is agricultural as it is here. There are lots of fireflies here but none there. I can't chalk it up to dry and intense heat because my friend Sue, in Texas, has lots of fireflies. I really have no idea. It's one of life's little mysteries. But now, the June nights have become special to me like that crossroad back home and whenever I see a firefly, I must smile. They are like a nighttime wink reminding me that life is always an exciting adventure and I sure won't argue with that.

I've had my share of adventures since landing here, some dramatic like climbing into a cotton picker and some quiet and close to the earth like the first time I discovered we had little brown frogs in our yard. That was pretty cool for me and I would have loved sharing that moment with my grandsons. They would have been wowed right along with their Grandma.

July 23, 2018 - Blessings

There are few things that make a Catholic more curious than who a new, incoming priest will be. With Fr. Jarek, of Sacred Heart parish, going on sabbatical this year, after Easter, we knew two things. We knew we would have substitute priests all summer and we didn't know if Father Jarek, after 9 years, would be reassigned to us upon his return. It's not always easy being a Catholic parish in a southern rural community so, generally, change isn't welcomed. It was difficult enough having to share Fr. Jarek with the church in New Madrid but having to share a potential unknown made it even more difficult.

In California, the sharing of a priest isn't at all typical. It's not unheard of but it's not typical. A higher population equals a higher number of Catholics through the state which means a higher number of priests, both homegrown and from elsewhere. The numbers aren't nearly as high as those prior to the turbulent 60s and the winds of change 70s, but high enough that most parishes had their own priest(s). Not so in Missouri.

We Catholics, in Missouri, are either clustered in large urban centers or spread out over wide geographic areas. It also isn't unusual for a priest to cover two or more parishes. I can think of at least one priest who covers five small parishes. Needless to say, the man is spread thin. But, the low number of priests in Missouri is not the topic here. No, the topic this week is about what a Blessing they are. In the past twelve weeks that Fr. Jarek has been absent we have been blessed with not one, not two, but three remarkable men of God.

Our first temporary priest was Fr. Samsom who was from elsewhere in Missouri via Haiti. A man of infectious laughter and humor, his tri-lingual accent was a serious challenge to us. But, despite his Creole French, Spanish, and English being at war with each other, in the few short eight weeks, he was with us, his English improved in leaps and bounds. The key was getting him to slow down and certain parishioner weren't shy about showing him the way. Consequently, we heard stories of Haiti over many evening meals two to three nights a week. We discovered Haitian history from the point of view of the Haitian people and found it quite at odds with what we thought was true. We learned of missionary experiences in Africa and Venezuela, heard stories of language and custom encounters that were, to say the least, hair-raising. I'll never forget the night at Little Pizza Heaven when a woman who recognized his French accent and greeted him with a "bonjour". Before our eyes, we watch them become temporary best friends, bound together as they were by a common language, something that none of us could offer him.

It's always a mystery who is going to be assigned when a priest goes elsewhere. Our current priest, Fr. Dominic was another complete surprise. Born in Nigeria and arriving in St. Louis, in his early twenties, his command of English is impeccable. This isn't surprising since English is the national language of Nigeria. Yes, there are many tribal languages, but everyone speaks English. One very attentive 7-year-old exclaimed after Mass one Sunday, that he could understand him. Leave it to a 7-year-old to blurt it out in pure innocence and delight. It was a sweet moment. Though not as social a man as Fr. Samsom, Fr. Dominic is young, friendly, and knows how to send a great message. We Catholics like that. It's important to not only hear the gospel of the day but also to hear a homily that connects the readings and gospel and shows their relevance to modern life. We have the blessing of Fr. Dominic for a couple more weeks and I, for one, will be very tuned in to what this young man has to say.

This past weekend we were treated to our third blessing, Fr. Bill Spencer, a Franciscan missionary, both in the USA and internationally. Anyone who might have spotted him around this weekend would have immediately recognized what he was as he wore the traditional brown robe, roped belt, and sandals of a Franciscan Friar. Think "Friar Tuck" and you would have seen our man. He grew up in NE Louisiana where, at the time, 1/10th of one percent of the population was Catholic. Suffice it to say that growing up Catholic in northeast Louisiana, at that time, was interesting. Fr. Bill had already been scheduled to make a mission appeal at our parish, so Fr. Dominic was elsewhere, and we got a taste of where we fit into the role of a shepherd. It isn't just the priests and higher-ups guiding their flocks; it is us, as well. We are all called to be shepherds to each other and his homily from St. Paul clearly showed us the connection and the message. It wasn't until the end that he slipped in his mission appeal and hoped we would be generous with this small opportunity to, for a moment, be a shepherd to the world.

I love it when a priest leaves us laughing. Between sharing war stories about quitting smoking and not drinking coffee anymore, everyone acknowledged that Franciscans also make the best craft beers and ales around. Conversation at donuts and coffee after Mass was lively and filled with laughter. Fr. Bill fit my idea of a friar. Not only did he remind me of Friar Tuck visually, he also reminded me of Tuck's heart, brave, true, and filled with courage, characteristics I have always associated with Franciscans.

So, these past many weeks have been exciting for us. We have been treated to stories of danger and suspense, thrills and chills, drama, history, and humorous stories of unexpected encounters and misunderstandings based on language confusion and lack of awareness of social customs. It has been a lively and blessed time. All that worry and fretting was for nothing. Three men came to bat. We scored three home runs. It's been a great summer.

August 5, 2018 - A Year Later

It's been a little over a year since we moved here and the "firsts" that came at me so quickly have given way to a feeling of settling in and finding my comfort zone. Last year we went to the Backyard BBQ down on the river and knew few people. This year we were working at the economic development booth with Mayor Sue.

Attending city council meetings opened doors to avenues for community involvement and "getting to know you" opportunities. In between experiencing countless new life experiences, I also joined a book club, a garden club, and the Lions Club. I agreed to serve on the RSVP board (Retired Seniors Volunteer Board); the Pirate joined too, and he joined the Salvation Army board. We both pushed for fundraising for the county's General Education Degree program, with modest success. He joined American Legion and started attending two different Morning Prayer groups, one at the Methodist Church and the other at H.S. Smith Funeral Home.

Change has loomed large over our household. Don trucked forward with personal projects but overall for me it was a lot harder. In recent days, I've thrown a bit of a pity party for myself as I struggled to put my old life behind me. Certain people in my immediate circle (yes, surprisingly, I made a circle of friends - no small feat at 70) will testify to that. But I got through it and rediscovered, yet again, that life never, ever stands still.

The thing that got me going in the right direction again was reactivating my daily prayer life. There's nothing like reconnecting with God's friendship to clear the cobwebs of confusion that can cloud the mind. Change is God's challenge to me to look forward, not backward. It's His challenge to me to keep the good memories of the past *in* the past.

Anne Jeffries

Change is never easy, especially when it sneaks up on you. Today is certainly that kind of day. Today we learned at church that our much-loved Fr. Jarek would not be returning to us now that his sabbatical is completed. While we wish him well on the next path of his priesthood, we also know that our small Catholic community is in for a change. Change will be harder for some than for others but it's our job as members of our parish community to help and support those who will have a hard time dealing with change. It is also our job to welcome our new and young priest, Fr. Dominic, to the community since he was no doubt as surprised by the assignment as we were by the loss of Fr. Jarek.

I've learned a lot about change this past year and I'm grateful to have found a way back to my prayer life. It arrived just in time.

At this point now, California Girl will start appearing more intermittently. The learning curve of small-town living has peaked, and I seem to have landed in a comfort zone much to my liking. The past is in the past and my present reality is finding a pace that is comfortable and keeps me moving forward and looking outward. There will always be something for me to say and I won't be shy about sharing it here. You've all been so warm and kind since our arrival and that has made it very easy for me to find my place in the fabric of the community of Caruthersville.

Afterword

Life has quieted for me in my second year here. It has slowed down considerably, and progress, of a sort, has been made.

- After nine years of retirement, I'm working again, part-time.
- I've taken up yoga.
- I'm a singing regular on Little Pizza Heaven music nights singing *California Dreaming*.
- I have become acquainted with sinkholes.
- Much to my surprise, I started painting again
- My driving comfort zone has extended to Kennett.
- This book happened.
- And, no, my room upstairs has not been finished yet. But I found someone who is a wiz at organizing. Help is on the way.

Life is good.